How to become a professional

Life
COACH

by Wayne Malcolm

MINISTRY IN ART PUBLISHING
communicating excellence

Ministry In Art Publishing Ltd
email publishing@ministryinart.com
www.miapublishing.com

This publication is designed to provide accurate and authoritative
information in regard to the subject matter covered. It is sold with the
understanding that the publisher is not engaged in rendering legal,
accounting, or other professional service. If legal advice or other
expert assistance is required, the services of a competent professional
should be sought.

ISBN: 978-0-9551496-6-5

Cover design by Allan Sealy
www.miadesign.com

Table of contents

Introduction

Life coaching is the business opportunity of the decade. How many people do you know right now that are dissatisfied with their life? Go ahead and ask them. You'll find out that most people are looking for a way to change their lives in most areas, if not altogether.

There are four things that we are all pursuing in one way or another; four things that we all need in order to feel whole and happy in life. They are:

- Fulfilling relationships
- Health and fitness
- Career success and satisfaction
- Inner peace and fulfilment

There is not one person out there that isn't looking for major improvements in one or all of these four areas. The problem is that...

Changing your life takes real work...

In the form of:

Self analysis – an honest look at where you are in relation to where you want to be

Goal setting – setting targets for yourself in all the key areas

Planning – Developing a flexible and reliable plan for attaining your goals

Motivation – Keeping yourself going when you don't feel like it

Time management – creating time to achieve your goals without jeopardising your responsibilities

Problem solving – tackling obstacles in your way so that you can move on

Self-assessments – monitoring your progress in a systematic and objective way so that you can quickly identify problems or reward yourself for reaching your targets.

What if you could master these seven simple techniques?

Then you could help almost anyone to improve his or her own quality of life in all four key areas.

With your help, virtually anyone can

- Improve the quality of their relationships (or find new ones),
- Improve their overall health and fitness,
- Experience total job satisfaction and career success
- Find inner peace and personal fulfilment.

Although most people know this, they would not do it without the help of a life coach. That is why life coaching has become the business opportunity of the decade.

Would you make a good Life Coach?

If you are the kind of person that:

Regularly gives advice to family and friends
Is usually there to support people through a crisis
Feels compelled to help when someone is in need
Understands a thing or two about life and living
Have achieved something yourself that required great
discipline

Then you could be the next big thing in Life Coaching!

You can take your natural inclinations and turn them into
a full or part-time business as a professional life coach.

But don't I need years of training and qualifications?

Absolutely not! Although life coaching is internationally
recognised as a reputable profession, there is at present
no international standard or governing body for the
practise. This is because what makes a life coach
effective is the results they get. Of course, there are some
basics, some tools and some rules of the trade. But once
these are learnt and mastered, you are ready to begin a
potentially lucrative career helping others to find
fulfilment, success and happiness in life.

Job satisfaction?

Imagine being paid to:

- Help others achieve their relationship goals
- Help others achieve their health and fitness goals
- Help others achieve their business and career goals
- Help others achieve their spiritual and inner
  world goals

Imagine that! You would literally be in the business of putting smiles on people's faces.

The Personal Development Industry

The personal development industry is a multi-trillion dollar industry that is growing exponentially around the world as more people are trying to live longer, healthier, richer and more fulfilling lives. They are also willing to pay for products or services that will assist and advance their quest for time, money, physical and inner freedom. Consequently:

The Nutrition business is booming into the trillions.
Professional development seminars are sold out.
Wealth creation books and audio programmes have sold for **billions.**

Self-help and DIY everything is now available everywhere.

The question is - how do you get into this high growth industry?

The traditional route into this industry is called **expertise**. You had to develop expertise and a reputation over many years in a particular field before you could begin speaking professionally, coaching or marketing self-help products. However, today all that is past! The fast track into the personal development industry is to borrow somebody's expertise, experience and reputation.

ICAN help!

I developed the **ICAN life coaching system** as the result of my experience as a pastor, counsellor and life coach over many years. Along with my experience, I have spent the last seven years researching the field extensively in order to include the very latest coaching concepts and strategies from leading experts.
 It has been my privilege to coach hundreds of people from all walks of life into personal fulfilment and success.

ICAN - get you started in business as A Professional Life Coach!

The great news for you is that I have summarised my strategies and philosophy in this book that you are now holding so that what took me seven years to discover can be yours with some basic reading and practice.

In this book you'll learn:

The Basics

What Life Coaching is?

- How Life Coaching differs from traditional counselling, teaching, mentoring or therapy

- The characteristics and competences of a good Coach

- The international coaching code of ethics

- Good coaching practise

- The logistics of coaching at venues, by telephone, online or in group settings.

- How to write coaching contracts and agreements

The Skills

- How to assess a clients needs
- How to set SMART goals
- How to convert goals into plans
- Strategies for effective time management
- Strategies for effective problem solving
- Strategies for effective mood management
- Strategies for effective communication

- Three techniques for motivating clients
- Models for behavioural change

The Business

- How to market your services
- How to promote and advertise your services
- How to sell your services
- How to set up your business as a professional life coach
- The legal compliances and insurance options for coaching professionals

PART I
COACHING BASICS

Chapter 1
The Basics

A Life coaching definition

Life coaching is a concept embodying several approaches to success. Success, in this context means achieving your goals without violating your values. Coaching does not view success in terms of modern success symbols; instead it evaluates success in terms of what a client wants to achieve. The common denominator in all coaching schools and perspectives is the idea of partnerships. The coach becomes part of the client's team and works alongside them to fulfil their aspirations. Success for the coach is success for the client. This means that a coach is only successful in as much as their clients achieve their goals. The client remains the subject of the coaching partnership whilst success remains the object of it.

Because life coaching embodies various disciplines, practises and approaches to success, I am yet to read of one definition that satisfies all camps. I am therefore going to offer three definitions in the knowledge that some coaching schools won't be impressed:

- Life coaching is a partnership between a coach and a client for the purpose of realising the client's personal and professional goals.

- Life coaching is the process of enabling behavioural change in clients using coaching techniques and tools, whilst providing accountabilities for the process.

- Life coaching is the practise of assisting others to: clarify their goals, make value-based decisions, develop action plans and acquire the necessary life skills for the attainment of their goals, whilst providing support, motivation and accountability for the whole process.

A life coach is an expert

A life coach is an expert in the science and process of behavioral change. They can help you to make the changes you need in order to get the results you want. They may not be able to advise clients unless they are using the directive coaching approach. If their coaching style is non-directive, they will usually be unwilling to offer advice. Their expertise is in enabling change.

There is a difference between circumstantial change and behavioral change. A coach will enable you to change your circumstances (domestic, financial, career, performance etc), by enabling you to change your own behavioral patterns and cycles. Behavior, in the coaching context includes internal behaviors such as thoughts and feelings as well as external behaviors like words and deeds. A life coach uses tools and techniques that are proven to enable change.

A history of coaching

The word 'coach' first appeared in the English language around the year 1500 and was used to describe a particular form of carriage for transportation. In the 1850s, the word 'coach' was used by English universities to describe the person who helped students prepare for exams. Coaching appears in management literature in the 1950s and was used to describe a management skill. Life skills coaching began in New York as an educational programme for under privileged kids in the 1960s. The programme was enhanced (problem solving skills were added) and taken to Canada where life skills coaching and business coaching fused. From this base, coaching became widely acknowledged as a profession with training and credentials for coaches. In spite of this, coaching did not receive much attention from the business community until the 1980s when the idea of executive coaching emerged.

The difference between Life coaching and therapy

Life coaching differs from counselling, psychotherapy and mentoring in several ways:

- Life coaching differs from counselling and therapy in that it focuses exclusively on the clients potential and not on their past problems. In this respect it is future oriented and does not attempt to fix the past.

- Life coaches do not solve problems for people or make decisions for them. Rather, they use techniques and models that enable clients to make decisions and solve problems for themselves. Coaches do not change people; they enable change.

- Life coaching differs from mentoring in that the coach may never have personally obtained what the client hopes to achieve. The mentor trains from example, experience and expertise. The coach's expertise lies in enabling behavioural change.

The link between life coaching and sports psychology

Life coaching utilises the principles of sports psychology but not all the practises. Top athletes use coaches to take them beyond past limitations and boundaries and to unleash their full potential. This principle holds true in life coaching. Although some sports coaches have been known to use aggression and anger when coaching athletes (a strategy that life coaches seldom employ), the basic goal is to:

- Help the athlete clarify values
- Set challenging goals
- Visualise outcomes
- Overcome self limiting beliefs
- Employ winning strategies for success.

Who needs life coaching?

The Life Coach works with individuals who want to:

- Change and grow
- Restructure and improve their lives

- Work through transitions
- Find fulfilment
- Achieve balance

What are the main benefits you can get from Life coaching?

The main benefits of life coaching come in the form of the three C's, which are: Clarity, Control and Confidence

A.   **Clarity**. You will come out of a good life coaching experience with absolute clarity about: what is important to you in life, what you want to achieve, what you want to become, why you want what you want and how you intend to get it.

B.   **Control.** You will come out of a good life coaching experience with greater control over the critical factors in your life including: your time, your health, your mind, your money, your relationships, your career, your overall direction - including your personal, social and professional life.

C.   **Confidence.** You will come out of a good life coaching experience with increased self esteem and greater self-confidence. This in turn leads to increased productivity, better performance and an overall sense of competence.

What kind of person uses a life coach?

One of the great lessons that we learn for the world of sports is that WINNERS EMPLOY COACHES AND LOSERS DO NOT! If an athlete or team is determined to win, one of the first things they do is look for a great coach: someone that can help them develop a winning strategy, sharpen their skills and support them in training as well as in competition. The same principle holds true in life.

Winners usually win because they develop around them a winning team. You have heard the saying: 'It takes team work to make the dream work.' Well, it is true no matter what the dream is. You may already have an accountant, a lawyer, a financial advisor or a fitness instructor on your team; but when you bring a life coach on board, it puts you in the league of some of the most productive and balanced people in the world.

How long does life coaching last?

The objective in life coaching is not to create co-dependence between you and your coach, but rather to kick-start your progress towards specific goals. For that reason we (in our system) do not allow coaching to go beyond twelve sessions. In twelve one hour sessions, all the objectives of the coaching relationship can be achieved including the diagnostics, strategy, skills and support aspects of your personal coaching program. There are exceptions to this rule. It may not be possible to see a result for six months or a year in certain professions. Likewise a client may wish to retain you for a year or more for support or a coach-on-demand service because of the nature of their goals. Each case should therefore be judged on its merits.

Are the results of life coaching measurable?

Absolutely! Part of the initial diagnostic analysis is aimed at establishing a definite starting point for the coaching process as well as the key performance indicators that tell both you and your coach whether or not you are making progress. Coaching is goal oriented. This means that you can determine the success of a coaching relationship by whether or not the initial objectives have been achieved.

How does the life coach work?

Your life coach takes you each week through a series of exercises designed scientifically to prompt deeper levels of thought and creativity. Each exercise will bring greater clarity, control and confidence to you concerning the future. These exercises are the tools of the life coach's trade.

When should a life coach be employed?

Life coaching is always a good idea. However, it can be a real life saver if employed at times of personal change. e.g.

- Career change
- Kids left home
- Retirement
- Divorce

- Moving home

This also holds true when you become aware that you need a major change of lifestyle e.g.

- Increasing stress levels
- Imbalance between personal and professional life
- Domestic tension
- Health problems
- Difficult decisions
- Before, during or after a crisis
- Redundancy
- Leaving university
- Bereavement Etc.

Each of these very real life experiences requires personal change management. Your life coach can walk you through that change in such a way that boosts your own self confidence and leaves you in control at all times.

How much does life coaching cost?

Quality life coaching is a professional service offered by professional people who are licensed and backed by a professional organisation. The cost of the experience depends very much on:

The service you require – i.e. do you want a standard 3 month intervention or a coach-on-demand retainer style relationship over a longer period?

How much work your coach is required to do -

i.e. how many sessions and out-of-session hours the coach is required to put in.

How much experience the coach has – an expert with years of experience and an established high-net clientele will cost much more than a start up coach.

How much is the coach saving your organisation – i.e. how expensive is the problem? A company losing hundreds of thousands because a key executive's personal life is falling apart, will often pay a handsome sum to fix or manage the problem.

Prices can range anywhere from under £100. per session at the lower end to hundreds per session at the higher end. Some are able to charge much more because of their unique niche and reputation for results. A good coach will always quote you for the service you require before entering into a coaching agreement with you. Usually a package can be tailored to meet your needs and your budget.

There are four types of coaching

Life coaching: This is all about managing personal change whether voluntary or involuntary, for the purpose of securing the best outcomes when in transition.

Performance coaching: This type of coaching

intervention is specifically aimed at improving professional performance and outputs by overcoming interference whether it is coming from a person's environment, skill level, beliefs or values.

Business & Career coaching: This is a directive style of coaching for the purpose of facilitating professional change and progress.

Executive coaching: This is about sustaining executive performance by addressing the executive's personal wellbeing as well as any personal or professional threats to the role. Sometimes it is an intervention designed to save the executive's job.

Coaching perspectives and approaches

There are three basic approaches to coaching, each of which is quite distinct and unique. They each share the essence of the coaching concept as well as the three main objectives of the coaching process. i.e.

- to close the gap between a person's performance and their potential.
- to enable personal or professional change.
- to bring clarity and greater awareness for the purpose of better decision making.

Coaches tend to fit neatly into these three camps and are often prepared to defend their particular perspective as being the most effective and the most authentic. This is a shame because clearly all three perspectives have a lot to offer and have proven to work for different people in different circumstances. It is a good idea to familiarise yourself with all three approaches so that you can draw from the plethora of tools available from each camp. The three coaching camps then are as follows:

Non-directive coaching

Non-directive coaching owes a lot to the work of Timothy Galloway. Timothy is the tennis coach who made some interesting discoveries about the way people learn. He documented his findings in his brilliant book called 'The Inner Game of Tennis.' In this book he shows that the chasm between performance and potential is often created by 'interference' in the form of self-doubt, perfectionism and fear of failure. He concluded that the external game was governed and determined by an inner game which, if won, would produce greater results on the field. Instead of trying to provide expertise, Timothy opted for inducing expertise from his players. The results were staggering.

Human beings are naturally creative and have capacities that cannot be fully exhausted in any one life-time. Non-directive coaching is all about enabling change and improving performance through self-awareness and greater clarity about the real issues at stake. By tapping into a person's natural creativity and inner genius, the non-directive coach seeks to empower clients to make quality decisions based on well formed outcomes that make ecological sense.

Directive coaching

Directive coaches on the other hand do give direction, guidance and motivation to clients based on their own area of expertise. Career coaching, life skills coaching and business coaching are usually a directive process in which the coach offers tips and techniques for achieving a particular result. The difference between this sort of coaching and regular counselling or mentoring is that the coach remains convinced that the best is already in their client and only offers their own expertise as a tool for getting the best out of them. Arguably, there is no substantial difference between this sort of coaching and mentoring or training. However, directive coaching remains an authentic approach for the following reasons:

- It is a goal oriented, future-focused process
- It is a partnership for the clients success
- It presupposes that the best is already inside the client
- It aims to elicit expertise and internal resources from the client
- Responsibility for decisions, follow through and success remain with the client

Directive coaching is the most akin to sports coaching of all the other approaches because it seeks to offer the very best ideas for getting the best out of a client when it matters the most. A good sports coach will:

- Give guidance on techniques
- Create a training and conditioning programme
- Participate in the development of the game plan
- Offer constructive feedback to players and teams following a game

- Offer moral support and additional motivation before, during and after the game

It is not possible to offer directive coaching outside your own area of expertise. A business coach without business experience simply doesn't work. Likewise a career coach needs to understand some facts about career management and change, CV's, job applications, recruitment agencies and the rest. For the same reasons a life-skills coach will need to have an advanced understanding of most life skills. The good news is that you can use your work or life experience to date as leverage for your own coaching career even if your experience was painful. If you have been through a redundancy or a divorce, you may want to focus your coaching career on that particular niche. The way to do this is to become an authority on the issues surrounding such circumstances through research and study. Then you can use the coaching techniques described in this book to officially launch your career as a life coach specialising in life after divorce or life after redundancy.

NLP

Neuro Linguistic Programming (NLP) has been called the new science of achievement because of its emphasis on modelling excellence and its detailed research into the structure of subjective experience. Developers and contributors analysed the mental strategies of high achievers and peak performers together with the building blocks of excellence so that they can be modelled and utilised by anyone. This branch of popular psychology offers a plethora of tools and techniques for building rapport, managing your state, breaking addictions, overcoming trauma, creating self-awareness and clarifying confusing issues. The science is evolving and continues to offer models and tools that enable personal change and peak performance.

NLP practitioners are not concerned with the content of behaviour as much as they are with the structure of that behaviour. Instead of focusing on what is making you feel depressed or optimistic, NLP looks at how you 'do' that depression or optimism.

This branch of psychology is based on a number of presuppositions, one of which states that the map is not the territory. This means that our reality is always an interpretation of the facts and never the facts themselves and that our correlating emotions are always a response to our interpretation of the facts and never to the facts themselves. Another basic presupposition of NLP is that the body and mind are parts of the same system so that any change in the one will affect a change in the other. NLP then, not only looks at the language of depression or optimism but also the very physiology associated with these states.

This sounds somewhat like cognitive behavioural therapy (CBT) because it is! NLP does not claim to be the originator of all of its ideas; it simply attempts to highlight what works. In this respect it is a salad of perspectives in psychology and psychiatry.

NLP has become the most popular approach to performance coaching because of its basis in science and because of its amazing quick fix solutions. Performance coaching seeks to enable managers and teams to reach targets and sustain outputs. It is also useful in sports and public performances. Of course anything that would enable managers to reach their targets and sustain their outputs is of interest to the business world. That is why NLP coaching is still the flavour of the month for performance related industries.

To offer NLP coaching you need to have an NLP coaching qualification.   This usually means doing your practitioner and master practitioner courses first. Then as a qualified NLP coach you can tailor your coaching career towards the performance related industries. Of course NLP helps in a number of coaching situations outside of those industries; so whatever your coaching niche, it is still a good idea to get some NLP training.

Chapter 2

The Characteristics of a Good Life Coach

Focus on human potential

A good life coach focuses on a person's potential and not on their performance to date. Instead of viewing the client as an empty vessel that needs to be filled with the coach's wisdom, a good coach will view the client as a gold mine, filled with an abundance of hidden treasure. A good coach recognises human potential and then uses proven techniques to manifest it.

Belief in clients

You will never get the best out of a person if you don't believe that the best is there. Belief in the client is essential to the whole coaching process. This single fact differentiates coaching from counselling or mentoring which tends to emphasise belief in the counsellor or mentor. The excellent coach sees a mighty oak tree in the acorn and conducts the entire relationship upon that premise.

Respect for clients

A good coach recognises the courage and determination of anyone that employs the services of a life coach. The client, quiet clearly, recognises the expertise and dedication of the life coach in offering and delivering an excellent service. The result is mutual respect. Mutual respect is therefore the foundation of the coaching relationship. Where respect is absent, the relationship breaks down.

Non-judgemental

Part of the coaching process involves identifying and clarifying the values of a client. It is not the coach's job to impose his or her own values upon the client, but rather to use the clients own values as the basis for developing life plans and strategies. If a client's values conflict too much with the coach's values, the agreement should be terminated. The initial assessment should qualify this matter so that client and coach can proceed to build a powerful partnership that produces results.

Ethical coaching

A code of ethics is a professional code of conduct designed to protect the integrity of a profession as well as the interests of all concerned. It lists the rules of engagement that maintain the industry's credibility and safeguards the trust that is vested in it. When applied to life coaching, the code of ethics protects the coach, the client, the commissioner and the profession from potential abuses of a trust-based relationship.

Why coaching ethics?

Any trust-based relationship is open to abuse. Each abuse of the coaching relationship not only causes pain to the immediate victims, but also adversely impacts the entire coaching profession.

Abuses of the coaching relationship

The coaching relationship is abused when:

- A coach breaches the agreement
- A coach places his/her own interests above the interests of the client
- A coach charges unnecessary or exorbitant fees
- A coach overstates his/her own qualification or fabricates a story in order to get business.
- A coach breaches a client's confidentiality

And such like...

Not a problem solver

Coaches do not solve problems for clients; rather they enable clients to solve their own problems. Coaches do not take credit for clients' successes or blame for their failures because coaches do not make decisions for clients. Success or failure is down to the client. Coaches offer models, strategies, tools and techniques for desired change. Clients choose and employ strategies with the support of a good coach which produce results.

A resource provider

A good coach is an excellent resource for his or her clients. A good coach should have current knowledge of the best products or services within the life management field as well as a working knowledge of the models, techniques and skills for personal change.

Knowledge of essential life skills

The essential life skills are:

Self discovery – identifying your own values, beliefs, goals, drivers & rules

Strategic goal setting – clear aims, objectives, targets, outcomes, purpose and goals.

Life mapping – developing a critical path and action plan

Time management – priorities, energy management & resource allocation

Problem solving – brainstorming, creativity & modelling excellence

Mood management – NLP, emotional intelligence, CBT & modifications

Self-assessment – personal feed back mechanisms and performance awareness

Communication – rapport, non verbal communications, negotiating, assertiveness etc.

Self-motivation – visualisation, anchoring, building momentum and refuelling
These skills are essential tools in the life coaching trade. Mastery of them is critical to the success of the coaching process. If you are serious about becoming a professional life coach, you should start by purchasing and studying a book on each of these subjects. As time goes on you should develop a library of resources in these fields so that you can operate as a flexible authority in each area.

Mastery of coaching tools

The life coach must employ proven strategies that enable change. These strategies arise from accurate assessments of clients' needs and the correct application of the appropriate life skills, tools and models. A master of coaching tools can apply the correct combination of techniques for each individual case.

Four communication skills

A good life coach must possess above average communication skills because the entire process will hinge upon four specific factors:

Building rapport – achieving 'flow' in conversation by mirroring and matching, bonding, blending and gelling with your client.

Strategic questioning – questions have the power to change a person's focus, frame their experience, access their creative mind and elicit powerful emotions. A coach must seek to achieve these ends by carefully wording and sequencing their questions.

Proactive listening – listening to both verbal and non-verbal feed- back, noticing what's important and noting change.

Constructive feedback – giving back to your client what they have said in a structured way that brings clarity and direction to the conversation and to the subject at hand.

Basic business skills

Life coaching is an established profession with professional codes of conduct and standards. As such it should be operated professionally and only by professionals. The professional coach is not only trained and certified but also possesses a degree of business acumen in the following fields:

- Marketing
- Promotion
- Sales
- Book-keeping

Each of these skills is necessary to run a professional life-coaching practise.

Chapter 3
Coaching Logistics

The coaching place
– venue, video, telephone

Careful consideration should be given to the place or mode of the coaching experience; whether face to face at a mutually agreeable venue, or telephonically, or via video link. Professionals who already work within a high tech environment will generally have no problem using a video link. The telephone may also prove convenient for some clients. Undoubtedly the best way to coach people through transitions is face to face at a mutually agreeable venue.

Working with a commissioner

The commissioner is the person or company that commissions and pays you to coach an employee. Some of your clients will come to you directly without a commissioner and others will be referred to you by their company or manager. In this case, your first meeting will be with the commissioner. It will be a free consultation with the following objectives:

• Assess the commissioner's needs
• Explain the coaching process

- Agree on your performance targets (what you are both aiming to achieve)
- Agree the terms of the contract
- Agree on ethical codes of conduct i.e. privacy of the client
- Agree on price and payments
- Agree on accountabilities
- Agree on the duration of the coaching relationship

Your commissioner holds the purse strings and countersigns your coaching contract. In this respect they are your client. Satisfying them is therefore paramount. The employee you are coaching may like you and perceive a real benefit from your conversations, but if the commissioner's needs are not being met, then the whole arrangement has failed. Once a commissioner is involved, you have two customers to satisfy. Occasionally, commissioners' objectives will conflict with their employee's needs, values and goals. In that case if their differences are irreconcilable, you should do the decent thing and terminate the coaching agreement on ethical grounds.

Working without a commissioner

In this instant you are working with one person because the commissioner and the coachee are the same. The one who signs the agreement and pays the fees is the direct beneficiary of your life coaching skills. Again the whole process should begin with an initial free consultation.

This meeting is necessary to:

- Assess the clients needs
- Explain the coaching process
- Explain and sign the coaching agreement
- Agree on fees and terms of payment
- Agree that life-coaching is appropriate for the client
- Ensure that both parties are comfortable with the arrangement
- Establish the mode of coaching

Clarity and agreement on all seven points is critical to the success of the coaching process.

The coaching agreement or contract

The coaching process should not begin until a coaching agreement has been signed. This agreement outlines the terms and conditions of the process as well as the obligations and responsibilities of both parties.

Price and payments

The two parties should agree upon a suitable package before the coaching process begins. The price plan forms an integral part of the coaching agreement. Typically fees vary from one coach to another. When a commissioner is involved, the stakes are usually higher because the company will have already determined how much they are loosing as a result of an employees performance. The cost of not helping their employee to get over a hurdle may run into the tens of thousands while the cost of an intervention may only run into the thousands.

If no commissioner is involved, then a person is paying

for it out of his/her own pocket. This should be factored into your price plan. How much work do you have to do anyway? There may be a lot involved in a particular intervention as well as a lot at stake. The important thing is to do your homework before quoting for the service. If a commissioner is involved, find out what the commissioner's budget is or what has been paid for similar interventions in the past. Find out what others are charging in that field. Finally, never quote for a single session; instead quote for a course. The benefits of coaching are seldom seen after one session; so plan for a minimum of four weekly sessions and then charge for that.

Coaching groups

When working with couples or groups, it is essential to obtain individual assessments. Coaching couples works if each is free to express their own values and ideals. Relationship coaching is a niche market that requires an additional set of skills and techniques. Life coaching is usually a very personal process. Although the process can be applied to teams, it then technically amounts to life skills training and motivation. It should be fully explained to the group that life coaching at best, is a one to one process.

The coach's tool kit

Life Coaches should keep a tool kit with them at all times during the coaching process. That kit should contain the necessary forms, articles, templates, information and guidelines for handling a variety of issues

The client's folder

Your clients should be issued a personalised folder including:

Completed and blank forms
A journal of progress
The coaching agreement
The coaching code of ethics
Articles
A resource guide

Coaching extras

You should develop a pool of free bonus material including, CD's, booklets and other articles that may prove useful to clients.

PART 2
COACHING PRINCIPLES

Chapter 4
Managing Change

Life coaching is effectively a form of change management, whether that change is voluntary through desire for a particular outcome or involuntary through a crisis or an unexpected turn of events. Although change is the most predictable feature of our lives, it remains the least anticipated and is seldom managed well. The question is not – ' will change occur?', but rather how can it be managed in a way that improves our quality of life and leaves us better off at the end. We do not have to be victims of change; instead we can become victors through change. Change need not be the enemy; it can become our best friend if managed in a way that works for us.

A life coach will often be employed during times of personal change, whether that is the arrival of new things or the loss of something precious. At such times people feel anxious, insecure and vulnerable. These feelings then affect their relationships and performance, both personally and professionally. At such times people welcome the support of someone who can bring clarity and confidence to the experience. Your job is to understand the complex and dynamic world of personal change so that you can coach your client through it in a way that enables them to make the change work.

Voluntary change

Voluntary change is easiest to identify because it is completely self driven. It is **desired change** designed to obtain something pleasurable or to avoid something painful. In this case, your clients want to change something about their personal or professional life and are serious enough to employ a coach to help them do it. This is great news for the life coach because it suggests that your client is already motivated and ready to go. The best way to support clients who want to change is as follows:

Help them clarify what they want, why they want it, when they want it and how they intend to get it!

What do you want?

This is a simple yet most profound question. Most people when asked this either look dumbstruck or begin to list the things that they do not want. It is important because of the way the mind works that your client is able to state what they want in positive terms. 'I want to lose weight' only tells us what you don't want and it further instructs your mind to focus on your excess weight. Unfortunately, we do gravitate towards the dominant picture in our mind; so it's really important that we change the picture. As a coach I would ask – "how much would you like to weigh?" I would then get them to restate their goal as follows. 'I wish to achieve my ideal weight which is…' Clarity about what it is you really want is a powerful form of motivation because it creates a target for your mind. To hit targets, you have to aim before you fire. In order to aim, you must have clear sight of your target. The clearer the target, the better your aim and the more chance you have of scoring a hit.

Why do you want it?

People often confuse the ends with the means. Losing weight is a means to an end, so is making money or getting married. The question here is – ' what are the ends that these means are meant to deliver?' Clarifying what your client really wants is critical because the 'means' don't necessarily deliver the 'ends' that they promise. Your clients may limit themselves to one particular strategy when a host of options that could deliver the same results may be available. By becoming clear about the ends or outcomes needed, your clients will be able to judge the effectiveness of the means they employ. If the reason you get married is to be happier and better off than you were before, then your marriage should be a means to that end and not an end in itself. Losing sight of this simple principle may cost you years of struggling within a mismatched relationship that ultimately makes you miserable and unhappy. The best tool for clarifying what your client really wants is to ask the question – 'if you achieved this goal, (losing weight or getting married) what would that do for you?' You can keep asking the same question each time they respond, until you strip away the veneer of their initial response to uncover what they are really trying to obtain or avoid.

How do you intend to get it?

The 'how' question is the most important question in change management because it taps into your creative capacity by accelerating the search for a way forward. The objective here is to create a critical path towards the attainment of the desired change. Your path should include action steps and tasks, milestones and measurements, resource management and accountabilities, as well as rewards for incremental success. Armed with a strategic action plan, your client will feel an immense sense of control over the future and will find in the plan the motivation to get the ball rolling.

When do you want it?

A goal is a dream with a deadline. Without a time frame your goals are merely wishes and high hopes. When attached to a realistic time frame, your goals take on a life of their own. They send signals to your brain which in turn begins scanning your internal warehouse of ideas, energy and solutions in an attempt to beat the deadline. You can help your clients by getting them to put dates on their goals.

Once the what, why, how and when of a desired change has been clarified, you can solidify the plan by having the client write it down. There is a difference between a plan and a written plan. Again, writing it down sends out another signal to your brain that says - 'this is serious and it has to be done.' The best way to write it down is in the form of a contract or agreement that your client makes with themselves. It could even be a simple letter written from the client to the client. It should outline – what, why, how and when a particular change is to occur. Your client can solidify it even further by posting it to themselves. All of these actions send powerful signals to the brain which in turn releases the energy and creativity necessary to make it all happen.

The final step in managing desired change is to initiate it immediately by taking action in either a big or a small way. Taking an initial action is the key to creating momentum. The law of momentum says that it is easier to keep something going than it is to get it started. For some people, a small step will start the ball rolling; whilst for others, doing something big will prove to be the winning ticket.

Involuntary change

This sort of change is caused by a crisis or a sudden turn of events. It could be a redundancy, a new job, a divorce, a bereavement or ill health. In such cases, change is imposed on you; but it still has to be made and managed. These seasons are usually charged with emotion and anxiety. That is why a good coach can offer real help by becoming that objective and pragmatic yet sensitive voice of reason. The key to managing this sort of change is to take ownership of it quickly by facing it pragmatically and deciding to get the best out of it.

Taking ownership of your change means turning it into a voluntary change that you can control! This is best done by making firm decisions as follows:

1. Decide how you want to go into it

With involuntary change, you often get little or no notice.

However, if you do become aware that a major change of circumstances is on the horizon, you should decide quickly how you will go into it by determining which state would serve you best at that time. Your emotional, mental, physical or spiritual state will be the single most important factor determining whether it is a change for the better or for worse, because how you feel and think may prove to be a bigger problem than the problem itself.

You can literally decide what would be the best way to feel, what would be the best attitude to have and what would be the best thing to believe when going through an imposed change. Simply ask yourself –'what would I have to believe in order to make this change work?' 'How will I need to feel in order to remain strong? Which attitude will give me the advantage at that point in time?' Once decided, you can then choose to feel and think this way. This procedure is then accelerated by you gathering as much information as possible about the change you are going through. With the information comes a sense of control and predictability.

2. Frame your experience

The language you employ at times of change has a way of framing your experience. For example, if you find out that you are being made redundant, you may begin referring to this as a problem or a crisis. By doing this, you put a problem context and frame around the experience, which in turn tells your brain that something is wrong.. When the brain senses that something is wrong, it releases defensive chemicals into your bloodstream which enable you for fight or flight. These chemicals create extraordinary stress and anxiety. You may combat this by choosing what language you use to frame your experience. Instead of calling it a crisis, you can call it a change or a turning point. Instead of calling it a problem, you can call it an opportunity or a fresh start. Of course language without thought is simply a noise. You will have to condition yourself to think of the situation within the context that you have given it. It is not enough to call the redundancy a fresh start; you will have to **think** of it as a fresh start.

3. Decide how you want to come out of it

Seasons change! You will not be in crisis forever! Even if you have recently been bereaved or divorced, you will not feel the way you do forever. So the first thing to decide is how long you want to go through it. Placing a time frame on your experience is a powerful way to control the experience. Further to this you should develop a fresh and compelling vision of yourself on the other side of this experience by determining how you want to look, sound, feel and be on the other side. You can then make it your goal and treat it just like a voluntary change.

Also you can decide what you are going to take from this experience into your future. We often take the pain of the past into the future whilst leaving the lessons in the past. Likewise we often take the worst memories into the future whilst leaving the best in the past. You should choose what lessons you are going to take with you and what pain you are going to leave behind. Likewise which memories you are going to take with you and those you are going to leave behind. If a painful memory tries to haunt you, simply scramble it. One of the breakthroughs in NLP is the fact that memories don't have to be painful; neither do they have to haunt us. They can be scrambled in such a way that they loose both bark and bite

(When memories bring pain, it is usually because of the way you remember them. You can disassociate yourself from the memories by watching them on the big screen of your mind as opposed to reliving them in detail. Whilst watching them on the big screen, you can scramble the sub-modalities of the images by changing the colour, size and sounds of the movie. You can further scramble them by adding weird music or cartoon characters. You can even make the screen so small that the image is barely visible. When you do this to a memory, it scrambles it and makes it difficult to think of in the same way. This technique can be used to leave painful memories behind).

4. The inner game

You are the architect and sole creator of your own emotions. Accepting this simple fact is the essence of emotional intelligence. Most people think that their experiences or circumstances are the reason for the way they feel. The truth is that experiences and circumstances have no power apart from the meanings that you give to them. The death of a loved one is painful because of what it means to you. Likewise a divorce or a redundancy is only as painful to you as the implications you attach to it. I have known several people who were extremely happy when they were made redundant and even those who have thrown a party to celebrate their divorce. There are even cultures in the world that view death as the ultimate experience of ecstasy and liberation. They feel happy for people who have died and look forward to joining them. The fact is that experiences have no meaning apart from the ones that we give them and it is the meaning of an experience that makes it painful or pleasurable.

Put simply; thoughts create feelings and not experiences. The way you think about a situation is the reason for the way you feel at that moment. The good news is that we can always control what we think. We have the privilege of interpreting our experience in a way that works for us. This means that even though we cannot always control the things that are happening outside, we can always control what's happening inside. It also means that the key to winning the outer game is winning the inner game. If you can control your thoughts and your emotions in the midst of change, then you can successfully control the direction and the outcome of that change.

Winning the inner game means competing successfully against doubt and fear. This is easier said than done because it involves a real struggle. The key to winning the inner game is to focus on managing your thoughts and not your feelings. This is because your feelings have no life apart from your thoughts. If you can change your thinking your feelings will change automatically. Managing your thinking during a time of personal change means three things:

Choosing your belief – whenever you feel bad, ask yourself – 'what would I have to believe in order to feel this way?' At that point you will start to identify the distortions in your own thinking. Secondly you can ask yourself – 'what would I have to believe in order to feel confident in this situation?' You can then choose a belief that works for you. Beliefs can be chosen and changed. A belief is simply a feeling of certainty. That feeling is based on evidence and assumptions that you hold to be true. In this respect a belief is like a table resting upon four legs. The legs of your belief table are the evidences that support your belief. By challenging the evidence and questioning the assumption you can quickly collapse the belief and replace it with a new one. E.g. if you believe that divorce means you will never find love or happiness again, then you can change that belief by questioning and challenging the evidence. You could ask yourself – 'is this belief true for everyone? Is there anyone out there that found love and life after divorce?' By doing this you will have provided evidence to the contrary. You can then choose to believe something that makes you feel strong.

Changing your self-talk – You have to become your own best friend. Often people speak to themselves in ways that degrade, dishonour and dismantle their very will to survive. This form of self-sabotage unleashes a torrent of self-destructive emotions. Instead, you should speak to yourself as you would to a best friend if they were going through a similar situation. You wouldn't call your best friend a stupid fool, or a waste of space; neither would you say they were ugly, fat, unlovable or unworthy of the best. Becoming your own best friend is a powerful way of managing your self-talk during times of critical change. Using this rule, you can quickly intercept any self-limiting, self-defeating or self-sabotaging conversations in your mind.

Choosing your focus – Your focus determines your feeling. In fact you cannot feel anything about anything you are not focused on. You may have had the experience of forgetting what it is you are supposed to feel bad about whilst having fun. You then suddenly remember and start feeling bad again. This is because you can't feel anything associated with it if you don't think about it . This also explains why so many people turn to alcohol in a time of crisis. The alcohol enables them to forget about it so they don't have to feel anything connected with it. The question then is – 'how do I change my focus without alcohol, drugs or casual sex?' The good news is that your focus can be changed together with its subsequent feelings through the power of questions. Questions determine your focus at any given time because they have the power to interrupt your thought pattern and get your mind searching other areas of the brain for answers. For example, when painful emotions bite, you can stop and ask yourself – 'what are the things in my life for which I am truly grateful?' Or – 'what do I have to look forward to in the future?' Or – 'is there a message from God to me in this experience? Or – 'is there an opportunity in this for me?' These questions change your focus and activate a different sort of emotion.

(NB: grief is a specialist area that requires another range of techniques. A life coach is not a therapist or counsellor unless they have been trained to do so. Coaching is future focused and goal oriented).

Chapter 5
The Structure of Behaviour

Why do we do what we do and what are the factors that control the decisions we make? This subject gets quite complicated when we consider the fact that people often act against their own better judgement or behave in ways that they themselves disapprove of. The reason is that knowing better doesn't necessarily mean doing better. It is as though we exist in different parts, with one part knowing what is right while the other keeps on doing what is wrong. Clearly our behaviours are driven by something more complex than a basic knowledge of right and wrong. Our choices appear to be the result of an underlying system made up of several components that work together to produce our behaviours, both positive and negative. As creatures of reason we are always doing what we do for reasons that seem good to us at the time. The question is – 'why do they seem good to us at the time and what are the components of our unique decision making processes and systems?

Although it is true to say that all behaviour is belief driven and that people do what they do because of their beliefs about what they may obtain or avoid by acting that way. It is simply not enough to say that beliefs cause behaviour. Many people continue to act in ways that they deeply believe to be bad for them or destructive. The opposite likewise is true. People often fail to act in ways that they deeply believe to be good for them. Clearly, our choices our based on something more than our basic beliefs!

I prefer to say that our 'belief systems' are responsible for our behaviours because a system is a 'combination of related elements organised into a complex whole.' (Encarta dictionary). This means that behind human behaviour is a combination of related elements. The fact that these elements are related means that any change in one element will affect a change in the whole system which must now reconfigure itself to work with that change. Another definition of a system is: 'an assembly of mechanical or electrical components which function together as a unit.' (Encarta dictionary). The relationship between each component in a system is such that any change affects the systems performance.

The big question here is – 'what are the components of our behavioural belief systems and can they be changed?' Coaching is all about behavioural change, whether that is internal behaviour like thoughts, feelings and attitudes, or external behaviours like words, deeds and performance. The coach's job is to enable meaningful and measurable change in the form of new internal and external behaviours that improve our overall performance. You know that if you keep doing what you've always done, you'll keep getting what you've always complained about. The simple fact is that to get something different you have to do something different; but to do something different you have to reconfigure the system that makes you do what you've always done.
This concept is a breakthrough because it suggests that our behaviour has a systemic root and infrastructure

complete with components that can be changed, replaced, altered and reconfigured. We can literally dismantle old and self-defeating belief systems and replace them with self-supporting and self-enhancing ones. It is not a coach's job to change peoples' belief systems, but rather to enable them to change those components that limit, restrict and defeat them in life and in business. You cannot successfully change a particular behaviour until you change the structure upon which it sits. This chapter is about how to change a destructive and limiting belief system into a constructive and limitless one.

Basic need

Human beings have three basic, fundamental and non-negotiable needs. We need them in much the same way as a car needs fuel, oil and water. Any deficiency in these essential fluids will cause the car to dysfunction and to break down. People dysfunction and break down when these basic needs go unmet. They are the need for:

- Security
- Significance
- Self-worth

To be more precise, we need to **feel** these more than we need to have them. It is not enough to be secure; we also need to feel secure. The opposite is to feel insecure. When persons feel insecure, they begin thinking and acting defensively and will often break all the rules of normal behaviour in an attempt to protect themselves from a perceived threat. Likewise, it is not enough to be significant; we need to feel significant. If a person feels insignificant they may become depressed and entertain escapist or even self-destructive thoughts and deeds. They may even resort to bizarre and outrageous behaviours in order to get attention and be noticed. Likewise, if a person feels worthless, they may lose the very will to live. The fact is that we dysfunction and ultimately break down if our basic human needs are not met.

With respects to security, significance and self worth, we are all pretty much the same. Much of our behaviours are driven by the need to top up or sustain these three elements. We only differ in terms of our beliefs about what will make us feel secure, significant and valuable. For the middle classes, security may mean financial reserves, insurance and investments; but for the working classes and youths on the streets in an urban centre, security may mean possession of a gun or carrying a knife. Also for the middle classes, significance may mean career success and a detached four bedroom house in a quiet suburb, whilst for a gang member in the inner cities it may mean winning a fight behind the pub. For some people, value and self worth lie in achievements and possessions, whilst for others it exists in relationships. In this respect we are all after the same ends. We only differ in terms of the means we choose to those ends. What differentiates us is our beliefs about what we may obtain or avoid by doing what we do.

The important thing to note here is that all behaviour moves towards a goal. That goal will be to meet a basic need whether it be real or perceived. Where as we cannot change a person's need for security, significance and worth, we can help them to change their perception of it and their beliefs about how to get it met.

Eight components of a belief system!

Our belief systems enable us to determine and choose the best available way to meet our fundamental needs at any given time. Of course it may not be the best choice when viewed objectively, but it makes perfect sense at the time when viewed through the distorted lenses of our own belief systems. Even the worst and most hideous crimes like murder, rape or genocide make perfect sense to the perpetrator at the time. They may later feel remorse, but at the time, they acted for reasons that seemed good to their twisted logic at that moment. So what are the components of our behavioural belief systems?

Values: Values are the things that are important to us. They are literally the valuables that we hold dear. They impact our decisions and choices in a powerful way by causing us to default to a decision that protects and supports our most cherished values. Furthermore, we all have a subconscious hierarchy of values, in that some things are more important than others. Most of our decisions are made in favour of our highest values. For example, if you already have nine speeding points on your driving license, then over speeding could lead to a disqualification. If you need your vehicle for work, one would assume that you would never overspeed again for fear of loosing your license. Whilst your license is important to you, you may yet break the speed limit if an emergency, such as an accident involving a loved one occurs. In this case it is not that your license or job is not important, but simply that your family is more important to you and is positioned much higher up in your hierarchy of values. We all have individual values and share the collective values of the culture and subcultures which we are a part of. These values create an internal default decision making response to choices. A good question to ask when engaged in a questionable behaviour is – 'what value am I trying to support or protect?'

Beliefs: By this, I do not mean what you believe to be right or wrong, but rather what you believe that you may obtain or avoid by behaving a particular way. It is well established that we are generally motivated by the pain/pleasure principle and that we are at all times seeking to obtain pleasure or avoid pain. However, we differ in terms of what we believe to be desirable and what we believe to be painful. The gang member who believes that violence makes him significant will choose violence over negotiation in order to settle a dispute; whilst the gentleman who believes that violence will further inflame the situation and ultimately cause him more pain will seek another option to settle the dispute. Resolving the issue is important to both persons. They only differ in terms of what each believes will bring about a settlement. A good question to ask when engaged in questionable behaviour is - 'what do I have to believe in order to justify this action?' Think about this; what might a person do presently if they believe that the future is full of pain or if they don't believe they have a future at all? They might act selfishly to get all they can now at everyone else's expense. In this case by changing their beliefs about the future, they can change their present behaviour.

Goals: By this I mean your conscious and subconscious aspirations and ideals in life. Where are you heading and what do you want from life? Everybody wants to be happy, healthy and wealthy. We only differ in our beliefs of what these things entail. In this respect, we all share the goal of self-preservation and self-satisfaction. Likewise, individuals have a vision or picture of themselves in an ideal state. That state becomes their subconscious goal and they will usually behave in ways that move them towards their goal. For example, if a young man sees himself as a top gangster in his territory, then becoming a top gangster will become his subconscious and sometimes conscious goal. If you encourage him to do well at school, he may refuse to make an effort because doing well at school takes him further away from his goal; whilst fighting, disrupting and disrespecting authority may take him further towards it. In this case, the faulty component is the child's own self-concept and image. The child clearly needs a new goal or set of ideals.

Drivers: These are the things that drive you. Again the pain/pleasure principle comes into play. Some people are primarily driven to avoid pain. Their goals and plans in life are all designed to avoid painful experiences.

If asked why you want to be rich, a person who is fundamentally driven by the need to avoid pain will answer the question in terms of the things they do not want; e.g. 'because I don't want to end up like my father.' Likewise, if asked why you want to be fit and healthy, the person may answer, 'because I don't want to die young.' Such language reveals the fact that this person is primarily driven to avoid pain.

Others are primarily driven to obtain pleasure. When asked why they want something, they will usually answer in terms of what it will do for them; e.g. 'I want to be rich so I can travel and explore the world.' These two sorts of drivers represent motivational directions. We are usually motivated towards (to obtain), or away from (to avoid). Although this is a general rule for which there will be exceptions, a person's language can quickly reveal their fundamental drivers.

Our personal drivers are the result of lessons that we learned from our experiences in childhood. We consciously and subconsciously draw conclusions about both ourselves and others from our experiences as we grow up. In this respect, our childhood shapes our personality and continues to impact our behavioural choices by getting us moving in specific directions. This information is useful for a life coach because it explains why some people seize opportunities (positive or negative) while others don't. It gives context to a person's behavioural choices. It explains why some people are risk adverse while others are adrenalin junkies.

Rules: We all have rules for ourselves and for others. They come in the forms of should do's and must do's. Of course, these are learned from the collective should do's and must do's of our parents, our cultures and our subcultures. People often do what they do because they think they should or must. We even fall out with people if they don't share or practice our rules. When people don't do or say what we think they should, we tend to get upset. For example, have you ever said good morning to a person in a lift? What should they do? Of course they should say good morning back or at least acknowledge you. If they don't we can feel offended Of course the best way to feel is curious and intrigued but never offended because we all live by a different set of rules and it is arrogant to assume that others share your rules or to insist that others keep your rules. Relationships work better with fewer rules. The more rules you have for others, the more there are to break.

Standards: Our standards are the levels of Performance or Attainment that we expect from others and ourselves. We use them as a guide and measurement for our lives. They are often the result of the collective standards of our peers. For example, if you often hang out with body builders, then you will expect more from your own body shape and strength than you would if your immediate circle were comprised of pub louts and beer bellies. Likewise, how you keep your home in a council estate will differ from how you keep it in a middle class suburb. What you expect or even demand from yourself is based on your belief in your own potential. The belief that you could be more, coupled with the 'experience of more' tends to raise the bar and create new standards for you. This is a great clue to understanding behavioural belief systems. Standards can be lowered or raised depending on the collective standards of your immediate peers.

For example, there is a reason why juveniles take crime to another level after coming out of prison. It is because they have been placed even deeper into the circle of significance that produced the criminal life style in the first place. Before being convicted and sentenced, the juvenile was already operating in a circle of peers that made him/her feel significant for breaking the rules and committing crimes. Now in prison they are thrust even deeper into that circle where new standards can be observed and embraced.

Knowledge: Ignorance explains a lot of human behaviour because it limits our options. When making a choice, you have to have a mental list of options to choose from. The more options available, the more likely you are to choose a course that works. The fewer options you have, the more likely you are to choose a course that doesn't work. People are only ever choosing from the options available to them at the time. If you don't know a better way to deal with a dilemma, you will choose the available option even if it doesn't work in the long run. Some people know of only one way to deal with a dispute; i.e. with their fists. Others may choose to talk, while some may just walk away. The difference lies in their own level of knowledge and skill in this area. In this respect you can change a person's behaviour by simply furnishing them with a new piece of information. This is why simple ideas can have the effect of changing a person's life. With new information comes new power to choose a better way.

Skill: Knowing what to do will not help if you don't feel capable of doing what you know. A person's level of skill is therefore a critical component in their decision making process. The more skill, the more options available! That is why new skills lead to new behavioural patterns and even a completely changed life. The persons who learn how to manage their emotions so that they can change the way they feel at will are going to make superior choices at critical moments because they will be able to de-personalise the situation and deal with it objectively. On the other hand, the persons lacking emotional intelligence will be more prone to jump to conclusions and react emotionally without thinking. Their temper, jealousy or anger will get the better of them. When dealing with persons like these, remember that the problem may not lie in the persons' values and beliefs; but it may be just a matter of skill. On the other hand if a person is emotionally intelligent but still chooses to express anger in destructive ways, you may want to check their beliefs, values, rules and standards for the fault.

Pain killers

Normal life comes complete with both pleasurable and painful emotions. We all have to deal with them. However some people experience much more pain in their lives than is normal. The experience of loss, violation, abandonment or serious setback can lead to years of pain for many who do not possess the skill of cutting off the past but instead are constantly reliving it. No one can live a normal life in a state of constant pain. When constant underlying pain is present, a person will seek to medicate it by indulging in any behaviour that takes it away even if it is only for that moment. Blatantly destructive behaviour is often an attempt to self-medicate an underlying issue. Until that issue is properly resolved, a person may continue to act against their better judgement and against their own values, rules and standards in ways that provide temporary relief from an otherwise painful existence. The main painkillers are:

- Alcohol
- Sex
- Drugs
- Violence
- Binging
- Working
- Deviance

When a person is hurting they think like this: 'the pain justifies the pleasure!' They claim the right to satisfy themselves at the expense of others with total disregard for the wider consequences of their actions. At the root of these coping strategies is a basic avoidance philosophy that refuses to deal with the issue itself. Counselling therapies and interventions may be necessary to break the cycle at this stage.

Addictions

Coping strategies usually become physically and mentally addictive to where a person feels that they can't live without them even when the underlying pain has been resolved. They sometimes have to go cold turkey and dry out in order to regain control. Although addictions and cravings can explain some human behaviour, it is important to remember that they sit within a context i.e. the context of those person's values, beliefs, goals, drivers, rules, standards, knowledge and skill! You can always break an addiction through altering one or more of the eight components of their behavioural belief system.

Low self-esteem

Finally, when examining the structure of behaviour, we must remember the power of our own self-concept. A distorted self-image is the cause of low self-esteem and low self-esteem is the mother of all behavioural dysfunction. Low self-esteem and even self hate is most commonly the result of:

Abandonment – either by a parent through separation, divorce, the bitter break-up of a relationship or even the death of a loved one.

Violation – when a person is violated by individuals who are supposed to value and protect them, they will often conclude that they remain stained or defiled by the experience. They can harbour feelings of worthlessness and total insignificance. They may even begin to hate themselves for what happened. Of course they cannot be blamed for what happened yet they remain angry with themselves for being in that situation. In such cases remember that:

No one can change the past; all we can **change** is our perception of it!

We cannot **forget** the past, but we can choose the way in which we remember it!

Breaking the rules – when a person breaks their own rules they can feel completely unworthy and even suspicious of any benefits in life. These people seldom question the rules; instead they question their own worth.

Not living up to your own standards – again the feeling of failure lives with a person who doesn't meet their own expectations. Instead of asking themselves how realistic this standard is, they ask what's wrong with me and conclude that they must be worthless if they can't meet their own basic expectations.

Conclusion

- All behaviour moves towards a goal. People act in order to obtain something desirable or to avoid something painful.

- The feelings of security, significance and self-worth are basic and fundamental human needs that drive us all. We only differ in terms of our beliefs about what will make us secure, significant and valuable.

- All behaviour is belief driven. However, a belief is a complex system of perspectives, paradigms, attitudes, philosophies, assumptions, perceptual positions, conclusions and ideas.

- No one can successfully change their own behavioural patterns without first changing the belief system that justifies it.

- Successful behavioural change is both measurable and sustainable i.e. it works and it lasts.

- There are eight components in a behavioural belief system i.e. values, beliefs, goals, drivers, rules, standards, knowledge and skill. These components are the same for individuals, cultures and subcultures.

- Change in any one component will effect a change in the entire system that supports a behavioural pattern.

- A belief or perspective can be changed by questioning, challenging and disproving the evidence that supports it. A belief is like a table, in that it is only as strong as the legs upon which it stands. The legs of a belief are the evidences that support it. Take away the evidence and the belief collapses. Collapsing a belief may involve seeing (visual), experiencing (kinaesthetic) and hearing (auditory) evidence to the contrary.

Checking the circuit board of your BBS

The following exercise is useful for determining where it is that a person is stuck. Many of your clients want to change but simply don't know how to, or are stuck in a self-defeating cycle and pattern of behaviour. You can find out where they are stuck by looking for the component in their behavioural belief system which is justifying the behaviour. The first step is to clearly and succinctly identify and define the behavioural pattern that your client needs to change. You can ask them the following questions:

What behaviour (not circumstance) do you wish to change? What do you want to do differently? This is important because it puts an outcome frame around the session. Most people think of change exclusively in terms of what they don't want which puts a problem frame around the issue instead of an outcome. Secondly, this line of questioning empowers the persons by taking their focus off the things they cannot control (circumstances), and placing it on the things they can control (behaviours).

Are you stuck on values? Is change important to you and if so how important? Does it even matter? If change is not that important to you then you can make it important by graphically exploring the consequences of failing to change.

Are you stuck on belief? What do you believe that you can obtain or avoid by behaving this way? Are those beliefs logical? Do they stand up to scrutiny? Is there any evidence you can present to the contrary? What do you stand to gain or avoid by making the change? Explore this and give it as much supporting evidence as possible.

Are you stuck on goals? What do you ultimately want in life? Does this behaviour support your ultimate goal or defeat it?

Are you stuck on drivers? Are you primarily trying to gain something through this behaviour or trying to avoid something? Can you avoid it any other way or can you gain it in a way that doesn't defeat your life goal?

Are you stuck on the rules? Are there any 'should do's' or 'must do's' at play here? Is there an expectation you have of others that reinforces your behaviour? Are your current rules helpful? Which new rules would serve you well?

Are you stuck on standards? Is this behaviour consistent with your current expectations of yourself? Are you operating below your own standards? Do your peers share your standards in this area? People seldom rise above the standards of their immediate peers. In such cases a new environment may be the key to change.

Are you stuck on knowledge? How much do you know about this issue? Do you have a list of options or alternative behaviours? Is there a knowledge gap or blind spot that limits your options in this matter? Your client may not know any other way of dealing with or responding to this situation.

Are you stuck on skills? What personal skills would enable you to behave differently in this situation? How would you rate your level of skill in these areas on a scale of 1-10? Fill in the blank: if I knew how to _____, I would be able to successfully make the change I need.

Chapter 6

Coach Tools and Models

Coaching Tools

Coaching is fundamentally a way of learning that consults the innate expertise latent within your client. The expert in any coaching conversation is therefore the client. The coach's job is to elicit that expertise and to induce a creative state in which the client can think clearly through the issues and act decisively with confidence. The client supplies the content for any coaching intervention, whilst the coach supplies the structure to the intervention. Since your primary job is consulting the expert within your client, you do not need to give advice, nor come up with answers nor possess any expertise in your client's field. In this respect you can coach an executive whilst having no knowledge of his business or role. Of course the more knowledge you do have will help, but it may also hinder the process if you are tempted to supply your expertise instead of eliciting theirs.

This point is fundamental to understanding your role as a coach. You specialise in change. You can help people make critical changes in whatever area using tools and models that are proven to enable change on any level. The principles of change are pretty straightforward.

In order to make any significant life change, you have to identify the what, why, when and how of that change. You have to be clear about what you are changing from and to. You have to be clear about why you want to change and what you hope to achieve by changing. You have to identify a path or plan for change and you have to set a deadline on that change.

These principles work with any sort of voluntary change. Some changes are involuntary and plunge you into a world of uncertainty; e.g.. a redundancy. If you become redundant, I wouldn't need to understand your industry in order to help you identify your options or to create a path towards the things you want. I only need to understand your business if I am going to give you advice. Since I'm going to help you consult your own innate genius, I don't need much information about the content of your dilemma.

The question is: 'how do I get you to locate your genius and then to consult with it?'

There are three specific tools that coaches use. They are:

- Strategic questions
- Active Listening
- Non-directive feedback

Strategic Questions

Questions have the power to both determine and change your focus at any given time. When the brain receives a question, it starts scanning the conscious, the sub-conscious and the super-conscious mind for answers. The trick is to ask the right questions in the right sequence. The right questions are those that get you to probe deep within yourself for answers. Questions also have the power to elicit creativity and expertise. In fact all inventions, innovations and other expressions of human creativity are the result of asking unusual or out of the box questions. Questioning assumptions, norms and mores lead to social change and innovation. Questioning methods, processes and procedures lead to business innovations and progress. Questions also have the power to change your state by getting you to focus on particular issues. E.g. if I ask you, what's the worst that could happen? That question will change your state and induce a number of defensive emotions. If on the other hand I ask you, what do you stand to gain? The question gets you focusing on gains and benefits and induces joyful and optimistic emotions.

As a life coach you must develop the art of asking deliberate, skilful and strategic questions which change a client's focus, elicit their creative genius and induce a resourceful state.

Active Listening

There is a difference between listening and active listening. Active listening is that which fully engages your physiology and probes the meaning of answers given. A coach will often be heard to ask 'how do you mean?' or 'can you explain that?' or 'please elaborate!' This is active listening probing deeper to induce deeper levels of awareness and clarity.

Non-Directive Feedback

The temptation is to advise clients and provide your expertise. This must be resisted as you are not a counsellor but a coach. As a life coach you must learn how to feed-back what your client has said in a non-judgemental way for the purpose of allowing them to hear themselves clearly. A good coach will be heard to say frequently: 'as I understand it, you are saying that...' or 'sounds like you are saying...' or 'What you've just told me is...' The purpose is to make sure that you understand what they are saying and that they understand what they are saying.

Coaching Models

As a professional practise, coaching uses proven models or guides to steer conversations in a specific direction. The direction is always towards learning. These models are scientifically structured to guide a person into deeper levels of awareness and clarity about what, why, how, when and where? The conscious mind has limits and can only process a limited amount of information at any given time. When difficult or complex decisions have to be made, our thoughts get jumbled, mixed up and twisted like a bowl of spaghetti. Good coaching unravels these thoughts and allows us to both think and see clearly so that we are able to make quality decisions with confidence.

A coaching conversation consists of strategic questions, deep listening and constructive feedback. You ask the question, listen deeply and then feed back to them what they have said. Feedback here is not the same as advise.

It is repeating what the client has said to you using a combination of their own words and yours so that they can hear themselves more clearly.

A coach does not seek to determine the content of a conversation. That's up to the client. The coach however must determine the structure of the conversation using a model or guide. Some pseudo coaches like to follow the conversation wherever it leads. However, a good coach would structure the conversation in such a way that it leads towards greater clarity and quality decision making. That is why these models are extremely useful tools for coaches. The most popular models are:

- The life wheel
- The ARROW
- T-Grow

The Life wheel

In the illustration you will note that a circle representing a person's life is split into eight segments. Some refer to these as the eight spokes of a person's life wheel. You may also think of it as eight slices of a pie. These eight represent:

- The eight components of a balanced life
- The eight factors determining a person's quality of life
- The eight areas of concern
- The eight areas of need for most people

The first exercise here is to ask your client to give themselves marks out of ten for their level of satisfaction or fulfilment in each segment. You will find that they will give high marks for some and lower marks for others. In this respect, their true wheel will not be circular, but will be rather an odd shape. By connecting the dots, you can get a clearer picture of a person's life and in particular which areas need attention.

The wheel acts like a mirror allowing a person to see a true reflection of where they are right now. In this respect it provides a starting point for the coaching process. If your client is seeking balance, this wheel can show them where and why they are off balance. It can also show them what to focus on in order to achieve balance. The purpose of coaching is to bridge the gap between where people are and where they have the potential to be. Coaching will synchronise their —

- Performance with their potential
- Address (life-location) with their identity (sense of self)
- Actuals with their ideals

This wheel can help to identify which areas are out of sync and where to focus the coaching process.

The ARROW

ARROW is an acronym for Aims, Reality, Reason, Options and Way forward. It represents the structure of an effective coaching conversation.

Aims: You can start this conversation with the simple yet profound question: 'what do you want in this area?' What do you want is a simple yet profound question because it seeks to identify and clarify a realistic target. All of the research into success psychology can be summarised as follows: 'people fail for lack of clearly defined goals.' Without a target you cannot aim, let alone fire.

Often, what people think they want and what they really want are worlds apart because they confuse the ends with the means. For example, a person may say 'I want to be rich.' This is clearly a means to an unspoken end. As a coach you would probe further by asking: 'and if you were rich, what would that do for you?' By asking this question repeatedly, you strip away the veneer of their desire to uncover what it is that they really, really want. This approach is used often in NLP (Neuro-Linguistic Programming) coaching where a person becomes aware of the core values and beliefs that lie beneath their wishes.

The objective here is to identify a clear set of goals/targets. For goals to be effective, they must be 'SMART GOALS' i.e.- **Specific, Measurable, Attainable, Relevant and Time bound**. Another way to think of this is in terms of outcomes. Your goal is to help your client identify and articulate a desired outcome. Outcome goals are the results of tasks or action goals and are not to be confused with the tasks themselves. For example, it may be a person's goal to start saving money each month. Again this is clearly a means to an end. The task-goal is saving, but the outcome goal may be to purchase a buy-to-let property as an investment for financial security. Whatever the case, you should not leave the conversation until clarity has been achieved.

Reality: In this part of the conversation, you leave the client's aspirations to focus on their reality i.e. where they are right now. The reason for this is so that they can get their head around the gap between where they are and where they want to be. This can be useful in terms of establishing realistic time frames for the changes they envisage. It may also help to identify roadblocks, limiting beliefs and other hurdles in their way. Your objective is to clarify to the client:

- Where they are right now in relation to where they want to be
- What is in the way.
- What, if any, are their limiting beliefs
- What length of time it might take to achieve their goals

A person's reality is both objective and subjective. It is both external and internal. Your conversation should probe into both realities. The conversation may start like this: 'so what's happening currently on this level?

Reason: We are creatures of reason who do what we do for reasons that seem good to us at the time. Your reason is your motive and therefore your motivation. At this stage we seek to elicit the motivations that lie behind the client's desire for change. Your clients' motive will ultimately be that they are seeking to avoid a painful outcome or to obtain a pleasurable one or both. We are all ultimately motivated by the pain/pleasure factor. What specific feelings are your clients seeking to avoid? What specific feelings are they seeking to obtain? You should also explore the pain/pleasure implications of failing to act versus acting. These are imperative questions which if explored will increase your clients resolve to take action and follow through on a plan of action.

Options: Now it gets exciting because in this part of the conversation we consider all of the possible options available to your client. Listing these options is a useful exercise for several reasons. On the psychological level, options put a person back in control. When you have no options you feel a loss of control and with it the accompanying feelings of anxiety, frustration and even depression. The more options, the more control you have. This exercise then serves to restore your client's sense of control. Secondly it serves to get your client focused on outcomes and not on problems. The problem frame (focus) induces an un-resourceful state, whilst the outcome frame uncaps your creative fountain and induces a wealth of internal resources. On the practical level, this conversation reduces the problem to size by creating a plethora of potential solutions. Your client should feel optimistic and enthusiastic at the close of this session and should also be in possession of a list of options. You should feel free to bounce around ideas with your client until new options appear.

Way Forward: At this point your client now has all the information necessary to develop a definite strategy and plan of action. From their list of options, they should choose and document a pathway from where they are to where they want to be. Their plan should be written like a project with definite goals, time frames and milestones. They can also factor in their own sticks and carrots, accountabilities and resource management plan. As their coach, they will be accountable to you. But it is also a good idea for them to share their plan with someone they respect. This will serve to trap them into taking action. It is a good idea and has proven to be a powerful motivator. For example, if someone wants to quit smoking, after developing a plan, they can increase their probability of success by sharing it with their loved ones. The increased accountability will serve as a powerful motivator during those moments of temptation.

Remember that the best plan of action is a proven plan. Modelling the success strategies of the successful is the undisputed formula for success on any level. Personal development and learning should therefore constitute a critical component in your client's strategy. This is simply the act of finding out what works so that you don't have to re-invent the wheel or risk failures that could have been avoided.

Finally, the law of momentum says that it is easier to sustain a motion than it is to start it. The hard part is starting. Your job as a coach is to go beyond plans to the point of action. Your client should take immediate action in the direction of their dreams. This can either be a small action or a big one. A small action should be taken before the coaching session has ended. However, for some people a big action will do the trick. Whatever the case, your client should do something to create momentum immediately.

T-Grow

The T-GROW model is very popular and very effective. It stands for Theme, Goal, Reality, Options and Way forward. The main difference between it and the ARROW is that it starts out with an identification of the main theme. A typical conversation would go like this: 'So what would you like to talk about with me today?' In essence the T-GROW model and the ARROW achieve the same result - a structured conversation designed to induce greater levels of awareness and clarity about a clients aspirations and perceived roadblocks.

As a professional life coach you should master your tools and utilise whatever model is appropriate to the clients needs. Become skilful at asking deep and probing questions. Don't be put off or shocked if a client doesn't wish to answer a particular question. Just work your way around it and make sure your conversations are structured towards achieving a result.

Chapter 7
Setting Goals

The main task of a life coach is to help clients to set and achieve meaningful goals. This requires some skill and an understanding of why goals do and do not work. Both classic and contemporary success philosophers agree that goals are the essence of and basic formula for success. Without them you are like a driver without a destination. You don't know where you're going, let alone how to get there, and ultimately you end up where you are. Life is quite circular for the person who has no goals. They are familiar with where they are, having been there so many times before. Instead of driving around in circles and going nowhere fast, we can break the cycle of non-progression and begin making steady and measurable progress towards a well-formed goal.

Four reasons why goals work

Goals enable you to aim before firing: It makes no sense to aim after firing and it's generally not possible to hit targets that you can't see clearly. Clear goals are clear targets. The clearer they are, the more likely you are to hit them.

Goals determine your direction in life: Where you are right now in life is the result of a direction you have been moving in over a period of time. To change your life you have to start moving in a new direction. The way to change direction is to identify a new destination in the form of a goal and then begin making steady progress towards it.

Goals have magnetic properties: Goals have magnetic properties in that they pull the best out of you and towards you. A well-formed goal will set your subconscious mind searching for ways to overcome any obstacle you may face in pursuit of that goal. In addition, it alerts you of any persons, opportunities, places or resources that could help you achieve your goal. Without a clear goal, these signals would be ignored or overlooked.

Goals activate mental laws in your favour: Clear goals bring with them clarity of thought and a resourceful state of mind. There are numerous mental laws that work for people who have clearly defined outcomes but against those who do not. All success philosophers agree that your state of mind and quality of thought are essential pre-requisites for success at anything meaningful.

Four reasons why goals don't work

Goal illusions: Unrealistic goals based on delusions of grandeur do not work because they are basically unachievable. Further to this, if your goal is unrealistic it will not induce the energy necessary to pursue it.

Goal confusion: General goals get general results whilst specific goals get specific results. If your goal is vague and uncertain, lacking definition and clarity, it will fail to pull the best out of you or provide direction or bring about the state of mind and quality of thought necessary to achieve meaningful feats.

Goal conflict: Often people set goals that conflict with their personal values. Or they set goals in one area that conflict with goals in another area. Such conflict is picked up by your subconscious mind and instead of generating energy and creativity; it generates procrastination and fatigue. For example, a person may want to spend more quality time with family, whilst setting a goal to be promoted at work. The uncertainty and internal conflict in such cases lead to procrastination, loss of energy and indecisiveness.

Changing GEARS

As a professional life coach your job is to help clients to set effective goals that work for them. The following is a useful formula for effective goal setting. There are many such formulas available from different authors and schools of thought. However, I have found this one to be particularly useful. I call it changing **GEARS** as follows:

G is for goal – first state clearly the outcome you desire together with the time frame involved.

E is for education – what research or learning would enable you to achieve your goal?

A is for action – List the steps you would need to take in order to achieve your goal?

R is for reason – State your reason for wanting to achieve that goal?

S is for success – describe what it would look like, sound like and feel like to be successful?

The GEARS formula is particularly useful because it defines what you want, when you want it, how you plan to get it, why you are going to pursue it and what it will be like to achieve it. You can now apply the GEARS technology to each aspect of a person's life. I call it the 8-GEARS plan!

Eight GEARS!

Love and family life – Goals in this area tend to cover three main areas. Either a person does not have a significant other and would like to find one, or they have a significant other and would like to enrich or even repair their relationship. Or they are in a relationship that they would like to get out of. In addition to this there are aspirations for our children and responsibilities towards parents, siblings and the extended family. Helping your client achieve clarity about what they really want and helping them to identify a path towards it is the job of a great life coach

Faith and spirituality – On this level people generally want to understand, explore, develop and enrich their faith. Goals in this area tend to fall into three main categories. They are knowledge goals (understanding/awareness), practise goals (doing them) or discovery goals (exploration & research). Whichever the case, these goals are born out of a sense of incompleteness. Helping your client identify the source and nature of this spiritual void as well as identifying a suitable strategy for filling it is the job of a great coach.

Health & fitness – Goals in this area are split into two main categories namely health and fitness. Health could otherwise be called wellness because it is both a state of body and mind. Fitness on the other hand has to do with physical shape and ability. Weight loss, toning, stamina and physical strength come into play. Helping your client achieve clarity about what they really want and helping them to identify a path towards it is the job of a great life coach.

Social/friends/recreation – A person's social life is an important outlet. Goals in this area tend to fall into three categories - A person has no social life but wants one; Or they would like to enrich their social life and enlarge their network of friends; Or they would like to scale down without losing out. Again, helping your clients achieve clarity about what they really want and helping them to identify a path towards it is the job of a great life coach.

Career/Job – Job satisfaction is important because a significant portion of your life will be spent at work. In this area people are either seeking to further their careers or to change them. Again, helping your clients to achieve clarity about what they really want and helping them to identify a path towards it is the job of a great life coach.

Personal Finances – Financial goals tend to fall into three main categories. A person is either trying to achieve financial stability, or financial security or financial freedom. The important thing to remember is that it usually happens in that order. Realism and honest assessments are critical. Enabling your client to identify a critical path towards their financial goal is the job of a great coach.

Personal development/growth – we all suffer from various skills deficiencies as well as blind spots and knowledge gaps. A great coach will help to identify those deficiencies and enable clients to create a personal development plan.

Contribution – The desire to make a difference, to add value and to make a contribution to society and the world at large is resident within most of us. As we become more stable and balanced, this desire will rise to the surface. Helping your clients to achieve clarity about what, why, how and when they intend to contribute is the job of a great coach.

The birth of a goal

All meaningful goals are born out of a person's values. That is why a values analysis is so important. Any goals that conflict with or neglect your highest values will create internal conflict and frustration. Your values then, are the important starting point in any goal setting exercise. Perhaps your most important goal is to bring your lifestyle into perfect harmony with your core values and ideals.

The three-phase method

Another useful formula for goal setting is what I call the three-phase method. It works like this:

Step 1 Choose one of the eight aspects of your life.

Step 2 Start with your ultimate goal in that area. This is a long-range goal and should be defined in terms of a well formed and detailed ultimate outcome.

Step 3 Then work backwards by asking yourself the question: 'What would I have to do consistently over several years in order to achieve this outcome?' These become your intermediary goals. They are mid-range and constitute your critical path or strategy.

Step 4 Only then should you write down your short-range goals by answering this question: 'what do I need to do straight away in order to kick start this process.' These are your short range immediate goals. They require immediate action starting today and lasting no longer than six months.

Step 5 What you now have in this area of your life is ultimate, intermediary and immediate goals. Looking forward, you have resolve, routine and results. Whichever way you look at it, you now have a three-phase goal. This level of clarity works for people who want to develop a five year plan or more. It is also useful to split a five year plan into 90 day increments. You can get a lot done in 90 days using the same three-phase formula. You start with the ultimate, use it to determine the intermediary and then use those goals to determine what is immediate.

Several keys will increase the effectiveness of a three-phase plan.

Write it all down – Simply divide a piece of paper into three equal parts and label them ultimate, intermediary and immediate. Or long-range, mid-range and short-range. Then fill in the blanks.

Identify a focal point - If you do this exercise right you will have a whole page full of long, mid and short-range goals. The key is to ask yourself what one thing would make all the others possible or inevitable? That one thing then becomes your focal point; the thing you concentrate on above all else.

Attach realistic time frames and deadlines to each of your phases.

Get out of the first phase as soon as possible – that means moving quickly into your routine and finding the rhythm of success. Your mid-range goals are all about rhythm and routine. The sooner you break into that phase, the sooner your results will appear. For example, if you want to become physically fit so that you can run for five miles and enjoy it, in the intermediary phase you will have to find a rhythm and routine that conditions both body and mind for that result. No doubt this will involve dietary changes and regular walks, runs, workouts and training. In the immediate you would probably do some research and take up membership with a health centre. Your goal is to get into the rhythm and routine phase as quickly as possible and not spend forever doing research or joining a gym. The sooner you get into your new dietary routine and your new workout regime, the sooner you will enjoy running.

Create a motivational affirmation for yourself in this area based on your ultimate goal. Affirmations work best by vividly imagining that you have achieved your ultimate goal and then articulating in a single sentence what its feels like to be you; e.g. 'I've just come back from a five mile jog - it feels great!' Now use this every time you train.

Developing a mission statement

A personal mission statement is the summary of a person's values, goals and overall aim in life. Your ultimate mission in life:

- Is about **becoming** something as opposed to achieving or possessing something.
- Must synchronise with your highest values
- Must maximise your potential
- Must satisfy you personally

When writing out your mission statement:

- Keep it brief – one or two paragraphs
- Identify your highest value
- Identify your chief goal
- Explain how you intend to achieve your chief goal

E.g. 'My name is Wayne Malcolm and my highest value is freedom. My main goal in life is to help as many people as possible experience emotional, physical and financial freedom. I will do this by first becoming an expert in this subject and then sharing my findings through books, speeches, seminars and other learning products.'

Developing a Personal Development Plan (PDP)

Your PDP is already contained in your eight GEARS. All you need to do is summarise their content on one page for your client. Often you will find that there are one or two core competences necessary for your client's success and you can focus the plan on those areas. You should then include a list of recommended reading and websites available from ICAN head office.

Designing your own future

By utilising these eight GEARS and their associated summaries, you can help anyone design the future of their dreams. The entire process can and should be done in one setting if:

- The client has been taught how to fill out sections
- The client speaks and the coach writes
- The client is pretty cognizant of his own goals
- The coach does not permit wandering in the conversation

Chapter 8
Life skills

There are four key life skills that the effective life-coach should master and be prepared to share with clients. Mastery of these tools can make the difference between success and failure in the matter of achieving goals.

Time Management

We all have the same amount of time to deal with, whether we are housewives or corporate executives. Even if our responsibilities double or treble in life, our time remains the same. We are simply given the same amount of time to get twice as much done. Notice I did not say the same amount of time to do twice as much work. Getting twice as much done is not the same as doing twice as much work. Actually, you can do half the work and get thrice as much done. The skill we must learn is the art of getting bigger results in less time.

Doing this means cultivating eight new habits:

- Your time is your life; value them equally
- Clarify and document the results you are looking for in a day, week or month

- Work from a written list of tasks.
  Write down your tasks
  Priorities your tasks as follows:
  A = important, B=good, C=nice, D=delegate or
  E - eliminate.
- Never engage in a B task until your A tasks for today are complete.
- Take the shortest route to the outcome you desire
- Delegate or eliminate any task that others can do or that need not be done at all
- Identify and destroy your biggest time wasters
- Pre-plan your months, weeks and days using an organiser

Problem Solving

Problems are both inevitable and essential in life. The first key to solving problems is to determine whether or not you have a problem at all. A genuine problem is anything that hinders your progress towards a specific goal. It is a road block, an obstacle in your way. If it doesn't stop you in your tracks just keep going. It may constitute a potential problem or even a smoke screen; but since it is not hindering your progress, just keep moving.

However, if the problem is genuine, you can usually design a solution by employing the following strategies:

- Define the problem
- Detach the problem from the rest of your life; put it in perspective
- Dismantle the problem to find its weakest link or the real problem

- Determine the outcomes you desire
- Write down 20 possible solutions to the problem
- Ask the experts for advice
- Employ a mastermind group
- Choose a solution and implement it
- Be flexible and willing to change tactics that are not working

Mood Management

We all get discouraged and frustrated at times. Sometimes it gets out of control and takes over. This results in days and weeks of procrastination and inactivity. To win in life you have to master these moments by learning how to awaken your most resourceful state instantly. This process is called anchoring. Anchoring is an NLP technique for relocating desired emotional states. Music is a good example of a powerful anchor. Often by hearing a piece of music that was popular in your childhood, you can instantly recall your emotional state as a child. The music takes you back in time, so to speak.

In the same way you can create an anchor to recall your most resourceful state, as follows:

- Relax and close your eyes
- Forget about all your cares
- Cast your mind back to a time when you felt unstoppable
- Remember it in graphic detail. See yourself large and colourful in the memory. Hear the sounds and smell the fragrance of that moment.
- Don't watch yourself from outside; remember and experience it from inside

- Now punch the air with your fist and say -
  'I am totally unstoppable.' Say it with feeling and
  deep emotion seven times

From now on your mind will associate the clenched fist
and the words, 'I'm totally unstoppable,' with the feeling
of total unstop ability. By simply doing this, you will have
created a way of relocating your most resourceful state.
Of course you can use any number of anchors. Music, a
song that you sing to yourself, a poem, an affirmation etc.
The important thing is to create the association in your
mind. You may need to do the exercise several times
before it kicks in.

How to use your anchor

- First recognise that you are in an un-resourceful
  state and will accomplish little in that state.
- Stop and activate your anchor as though looking
  for that unstoppable emotional state.
- When you find the perfect state, go ahead and
  do your work.

Employ the power of questions

Your feelings are usually the result of your focus. The
good news is that you can change your focus by
employing the power of relevant questions. To change
your feeling, change your focus by asking yourself some
highly resourceful questions:

- Who are the people that truly love me?
- What are my personal qualities and strengths?

- How many things have I achieved in the last two years?
- What exciting opportunities lie ahead for me?
- What people and things am I truly grateful for in life?

This simple exercise will change your focus from negative to positive and with it will come a wave of positive emotions.

Effective Communication

Communicating is understanding, and understanding is communicating. If we do not understand, we are not communicating. To be effective in communications, you should seek first to understand and then to be understood. Understanding effectively means listening actively as follows:

- Determine to understand
- Don't talk to yourself about other things while the person is speaking
- Engage your physiology and gestures in the listening process
- Look and sound interested and non judgemental
- Put what they have said into your own words and give it back to them so that they know that you have understood.

Being understood involves:

- Determine exactly what you want the person to understand
- Determine the exact outcome you are looking

for Say what you mean
- Be congruent in word, expression, tone and overall physiology
- Employ feedback

Motivation: Motivating yourself

Motivation comes from two words: motive and action. It means a reason to act. We can always find good reasons to start anything; but what we need is a good reason to continue in the face of merciless obstacles. The process of achieving goals can be quite painful at times. Whether it be the pain of discipline or the discomfort of the unknown, we simply cannot get the prize without paying the price. As a professional life coach, you need a reason to continue prospecting and providing a quality service to your clients.

The methods that you employ for motivating your clients will work for you. You can practise motivating your clients by continually motivating yourself. If it works for you, it will probably work for them. If it does not work for you, it probably would not work for them. So make it work!

Motivating your client

Studies have shown that we all respond to a preferred style of motivation. We are not all motivated by the same ideas. For example, a threat may have a completely different effect on you than it would on your neighbour. In the same way a promise may have a completely different affect on your neighbour than it would on you. Basically, it appears that some people:

- Move away from - Respond to threats or something to lose
- Move towards - Respond to promises, possibilities and opportunities

Some of your clients would have employed your services to get away from an unbearable way of life, whilst others would have been inspired by the possibility of personal fulfilment and freedom. When considering the three motivational techniques below, you should practise using them in both (away from and towards) modes.

Association

It is not the action that motivates us, but what we associate the action with. Never try to motivate somebody with an action or activity. Motivate them with its associated emotional consequence. The two emotional consequences of any action are pain or pleasure. We virtually associate all activities with one of these. We are either acting to obtain pleasure or avoid pain.

If the person moves towards, then you must link the action with pleasure. E.g.. By working from a written list of tasks, you will get more of the important things done and at the end of each day, you will not only feel like a champion, but will be well on your way to achieving your long range goals.

If the person moves away from, you must link the failure to act with pain. E.g. working from a written list of tasks is the most effective way to guarantee that you will get your most important tasks done. If you forget to do your most important tasks, they won't go away; but just carry over to the next day. At the end of the week or month, you'll be overwhelmed with important tasks that are as yet undone. Now how will that feel?'

When you are unsure of what motivates a person, just use both modes by simply associating pleasure with action and pain with the failure to act.

Visualisation

Visualisation is a powerful motivational tool that can also be used in both modes. This is where you get the clients to sit down, close their eyes and imagine in graphic detail what success looks, sounds and feels like. They should see themselves as having achieved the goal, e.g. weight loss, career satisfaction, a fulfilling relationship, etc. They should then be encouraged to feel the pleasure of success, to smell its aroma; to taste its flavour. You can then create an anchor for that experience by having them say with conviction - 'I can do it, I can have it, I'm unstoppable.'

If the person moves away from, you can have him imagine what it would be like to be in exactly the same place or worse off this time next year. Imagine the pain?

Affirmations

Affirmations are short suggestions to your subconscious,

which act as commands. What ever you repeat to yourself with emotion is eventually accepted as true by your subconscious and the process of materialising it begins. To make effective affirmations:

- Make them in the first person. Start with 'I am'…
  or 'I weigh'… or   'I have.'….
- Speak in terms of what you want to gain and not what you want to lose. e.g. 'I weigh 12 stones' - not 'I want to loose 2 stones'

- Speak in terms of your desired result, not the process. e.g. 'I am an expert in my field' - not 'I am studying to become an expert.'

- Write down your affirmation on small cards and stick them around the house, in the car and in the office.

- Repeat the affirmation at least 7 times throughout the day for 30 days with conviction and emotion.

- Tell two other people whose respect you desire, what you are affirming

- Keep pictures from magazines of people who are living your dream and write on them the words, 'that is me!'

Self – esteem

If you or your client remains unmotivated after use of these techniques, there is probably an unresolved conflict affecting your self-esteem. Explore this possibility before moving on with the following questions, but stress that they only answer themselves:

- Is there anything in your life about which you are deeply ashamed?

- Is there anything about yourself that you hate or seriously dislike?

NB: It is not important that they tell you what the issue is. Never ever press for the information. It is only important that they recognise that the unresolved issue is sapping away at their personal power.

If you discover that an unresolved internal conflict is affecting your clients' self esteem to the point that they will neither move towards or away from anything, you should:

- Recommend a resource; e.g. a tape or booklet
- See if it can be resolved by talking
- Focus on the future
- Use your three motivational techniques to move them beyond the issue

Selecting the right tools for the task

Mastery of these essential life tools will enable your clients to achieve any goal they set for themselves. The IA and the eight forms will reveal a lot about your client's weaknesses and challenges. You will discover that most of these are effectively a weakness in one of these four critical areas. It will either be:

- Poor time management
- An inability or unwillingness to solve problems
- An inability to overcome moods and negative emotions
- An inability to communicate properly with someone or a group

Once you find the root cause of your client's setback, you can apply the necessary tools by sharing one or more of these essential life-tools.

Chapter 9
Coaching Exercises

1. The wheel of life

This exercise is about life balance: Split a circle into eight equal parts representing the eight facets of a person's life. Have the client give themselves marks out of ten for their level of satisfaction in each area. Take the low areas individually and ask them what they really want in these areas. Take the high areas and ask why they think they are so high. Examine whether one strains the other. Establish what would be a realistic goal for life balance. Decide which numbers to raise or lower over the next 90 days. Draw an alternative wheel showing where the client wants to be in 90 days and make that the objective of the coaching course.

2. Changing GEARS in 90 days

This exercise is about action. Pick one of the eight life areas, or a subject of the client's choosing and put it at the top of the page. Discuss what the client really wants in this area and identify a realistic 90 day goal. Decide what education/learning the client will need to make this happen. Determine a course of action. Find out what the client is really trying to obtain or avoid in order to establish a clear reason. Use this for motivation. Have the client imagine success in this field until they can see, hear and feel it. Create an affirmation and description in the Success area.

3. The coaching ARROW hits the target:

This exercise is all about planning. First identify a SMART goal. Then have the client describe what is actually going on in order to add some realism to the goal and to clearly identify the gap. Find out what the client is ultimately trying to obtain or avoid in order to create motivation. Discuss all the possible options available to the client for achieving their goal. Choose some options and create a clear way forward with milestones and measurements.

4. The Problem Solver

Identify the problem as real and then use the 8D formula outlined in this book. Conclude with questions: 'Is there a need to consult an expert? Should a mind-storming group be assembled? Who might be in the group? What are the alternatives if this doesn't work?' Determine a strategy and then risk-analyse it.

5. The time flow Quadrant

This is a time management exercise: Have the client make a list of everything they do with their time over a given week or month. Include work, rest, chores and play. Estimate and write down the time each activity takes. Then place each activity into one of the four time quadrants: Urgent and important, Urgent but not important, Important but not urgent, not urgent or important. Then create a new page listing what the client wants their time flow quadrants to look like. Use the coaching ARROW or shift GEARS in 90 days to bridge the gap.

6. The Three-Phase life Plan

This is a life mapping exercise suitable for long range planning. Complete this exercise for each of the eight life zones in the wheel of life. First look at the long range and ultimate aims of the client by asking the question - 'what do you ultimately want for yourself in this area?' Then go to the mid range section and ask, 'what would you have to do consistently for several years in order to achieve this goal? Then go to the short range, immediate section and ask - 'what would you have to do in the short term in order to create this rhythm or routine?' When complete, the client has short, mid and long-range strategies for all aspects of their life. Find the focal point in each area and shift GEARS in 90 days to kick-start the process.

7. The self analysis

This is a self awareness exercise. Simply go through each of the seven components of the client's personality and discuss each one, writing down your conclusions as follows:

Values - what does the client hold dear?

Beliefs - what does the client believe fundamentally about themselves, life, God, others, etc?

Goals - what is your client aiming for in life? e.g. independence, wealth, family etc?

Drivers - is your client fundamentally seeking to obtain or avoid, and what exactly are their worst fears and highest aspirations?

Rules - discuss your client's standards for themselves.

Purpose - what does your client believe they are here to achieve?

Spirit - does your client possess spiritual consciousness and in what way do they connect to the bigger picture?

8. The Personal Development Plan

This is the creation of a personal learning programme: Simply compile the information gathered from the GEARS exercise and then determine the best ways to go about learning in these areas. Making the learning a main aim and then use the ARROW.

9. Your Mission Statement

This is designed to create a focal point for any life mapping exercise. It starts with the self-analysis on seven levels. Your statement should state who you are, what is important to you, what you want to achieve as a result of your highest values, why you want to achieve it and how you intend to achieve it. It should finally state something about your legacy and memory.

Or simply fill in the template:

My name is _____
My most important value in life is _____
My mission is to _____ *I will do this*
*by*_____ *In so doing I will*
_____ *and be remembered as the person*
who _____.

10. Affirmations:

Affirmations act like emotional anchors: The way to do this successfully is to imagine that you have achieved all your goals. Explore the sights, sounds and sensations of success. Then make a statement that encapsulates how it is to be where you are. e.g. 'I am the best in this business, I love what I do for people, this is not work but sheer entertainment!' Give a name to where you are mentally and emotionally as if it were a town e.g. "Greatsville" Whenever you need to relocate this state of mind, simply go to Greatsville and repeat the affirmation several times.

11. The prophetic CV

This is a vision casting exercise. Have your client write a CV postdated five years from now. Include everything from work to family, sports and recreation, personal finances and social life, personal development, contribution and love life. Use the wheel of life as your guide for what to include.

12. Checking the circuit

This exercise is based on the structure of behaviour. Whenever your clients become aware of a behavioural pattern that they would like to change, you can help them to better understand the behaviour by looking at each component in their behavioural belief system. This means looking at their patterns in light of their values, beliefs, goals, drivers, rules, standards, knowledge and skill. It should then become clear where it is that your client is stuck. This will start another conversation looking at that specific component to see if it needs to be changed or updated. Beliefs can be changed because they are not based on reality, but rather on perceptions of it.

PART 3
THE COACHING
BUSINESS

Chapter 10
Direct Marketing

The objective of all business is to create and keep customers. The entire process by which this is done is called marketing. Marketing is the process of identifying, locating, motivating and satisfying customers. Your successful career as a Life Coach therefore depends solely on your ability to identify, locate, appeal to, persuade and satisfy customers.

Identifying your customer

Who exactly would benefit from the services of a life coach today? For the most part they would be people who:

• Have undergone or are undergoing a major life change. e.g. new career, divorce, mid-life etc

• Are in high stress and demanding professions where work has taken over their lives. e.g. executives, professionals, managers etc.

- Are seeking to balance their professional and personal lives. e.g. athletes, politicians, clergymen etc.

- Are in pursuit of certain ideals including physical fitness, a degree or qualification, a fulfilling relationship, a new image, etc.

Locating your customer

Where exactly are these people? Where do they shop, socialise, eat, live and recreate? What clubs or associations do they belong to and what publications do they read? What TV channels do they watch or listen to and at what times? You cannot begin to promote your services until you have located your potential customers.

Appealing to your customer

You can appeal to your customers by promoting and advertising the benefits of your services. It is not enough to advertise or promote a service. You have to show the real benefits to the end user. The benefits of life coaching are numerous and are discussed in other parts of this book. Your job is to come up with a catch phrase or strap line that summarises the benefits of your service. E.g.

Achieve your personal best
Create your own future
Maximise the moment
From potential to performance
Create your own success
Enabling change

Tools for transformation
Generating genius
You can have more
The art of living by design
Bespoke living at its best

This catch phrase should then appear on all your stationary, your website and any other promotional materials.

Satisfying your customer

Your advertisement is your promise, but your delivery is the fulfilment of that promise. Any failure to deliver on your promise amounts to a breach of that promise and may render your future promises null and void. Because bad news spreads faster than good news, a bad service will destroy your business; whilst referrals from satisfied customers will build it. Your goal then is to deliver excellently on everything you promise. Customers expect to receive whatever is promised to them; but it should be your goal to amaze them by over delivering on your promises.

Beating your competitor

Finding out what your competitors are offering and at what price should form a major part of your marketing strategy. Nobody will buy from you if they can get a better and a cheaper service elsewhere. Your job is to make sure that they cannot get a better or more cost effective service anywhere else.

Your USP

Your Unique Selling Point is what differentiates you from your competitors. Your USP could include:

Price • Quality • Follow up • Efficiency • Free extras

When promoting your services, you should focus on the benefits of your service and the strength of your own USP.

Chapter 11
Promotions & sales

Awareness

Nobody will ever purchase a service they do not know about. Your job then is to create awareness of your service amongst prospective buyers. There are expensive ways to create awareness e.g.

- Newspaper adds
- Radio adds
- TV adds

These methods are the least effective in the business of life coaching because:

- None of them guarantee a response
- None of them can regulate the quality of response
- None of them can target your specific audience.

In the Life coaching business, the least expensive methods are the most effective. These include:

- Socialising with business cards in hand
- Leaving your business card in strategic receptions

- Referrals from satisfied customers
- Sending out letters to all family and friends, notifying them of your new career.
- Free seminars and talks

Each of these methods is relatively inexpensive, but will quickly generate awareness of who you are and what you do.

Advertising

Advertising is a direct appeal to a targeted audience to purchase your services. Whenever making a direct appeal, the golden rule is CLARITY. It should be abundantly clear at first glance:

- What is on offer?
- How it will benefit the end user.
- How to exploit the offer. i.e. by phone, online, written enquiries, etc.

What you should absolutely NOT do when advertising is:

Create riddles
Explain the features of the product as opposed to the benefits to the user
Make the contact details small
Focus on price as opposed to value

The features of the life coaching service include 3 modules - one on one sessions, forms and discussions. However, none of these describes a benefit to the end user. The benefits of the service include: Increased self –awareness, clear goals and vision, control of your time, improved relationships, balance between professional and personal life, problem solving skills etc. Customers do not buy features; they buy benefits. Your job then is to sell the benefits of your service when advertising or making a presentation.

Referrals

Your greatest form of advertising and promotion comes from satisfied customers who, if asked, will pass your business card on to their friends with a hearty recommendation. There are two main keys to a referral-based business:

Satisfied customers
Asking for referrals

The conversation would go something like this:

Coach:	*Do you feel that I have helped you towards achieving your goals?*
Coachee:	*Oh definitely!*
Coach:	*Can you name five of your friends or family that might also benefit from my service?*
Coachee:	*Yes I can!*
Coach:	*Would you give me their contact details so that I can send them a letter or give them a call, introducing my self and my services?*
Coachee:	*Sure!*
Coach:	*Would you also slip in a word for me, so that they are prepared for my call?*
Coachee:	*Sure!*
Coach:	*Thank you!*

Stationary

As a professional life coach, it is imperative that you operate and come across professionally. Part of this process involves the use of customised stationary. The most important pieces of stationary for your business are:

- A coaching license or qualification
- A customised business card
- A Customised letter head
- A small brochure advertising your services

The golden rule for business stationary is that it is all to be used for advertising! This means that anytime anybody comes into contact with any of your stationary, they should be able to see:

- Who you are
- What you offer
- The benefits of the service to them
- How to contact you.

All correspondence to your customers should be on headed stationary including:

- The initial letter
- The coaching agreement
- Invoices
- Receipts
- Statements
- Subsequent letters

Functions & Events

As a professional Life Coach, you should constantly be on the look out for networking opportunities. These typically come at functions and events where business cards are exchanged and new relationships are formed. E.g.

Conferences
Exhibitions
Seminars
Social functions
Shows
Awards etc

Your Website

A professional service requires a professional website. Your website should emphasise a professional look and feel as opposed to multiple functions. The more functions, the more expense. The key aspects of your website are:

- Biography of you
- Description of your services
- Benefits of your services
- Testimonials from satisfied customers
- Contact details
- E-mail link
- On-line booking form

Your website address should appear on all your stationary.

The sales process

Selling your service is not a matter of luck; it is a matter of process. You must become a master of the sales process in order to maintain a profitable career in life coaching. The process involves:

Generating interest
Making an appointment
Making a presentation

Lifestyle advertising

You can generate interest in your service by marketing, promotions and advertising. You can also generate it through your own lifestyle. By simply practising what you preach, you will stand out as an interesting person and effectively become a walking advert.

Making an appointment

You will not sell your service until you have been able to make an effective presentation. To do this you must make an appointment to see the interested party. The conversation may go something like this:

Coach: *Are you interested in finding out more about how life coaching could help you achieve your goals?*

Prospect: *Yes I am!*

NB: At this point the coach pulls out his/her diary and proceeds...

Coach:	*My presentation only takes half an hour. Wednesday evening is good for me or alternatively Friday Morning at about 10.00a.m.*
Prospect:	*Neither of those times are good for me.*
Coach:	*Ok! What would be a suitable time for you?*
Prospect:	*I'm free on Monday Morning.*
Coach:	*I may have to juggle some things around, but I'll do it just for you. Monday morning it is!*

The main thing to understand is that you never try to explain your services to an interested party off the cuff. You always make an appointment to see them where you can explain your services more fully. The main purposes for the appointment are:

- To sell your services
- To establish your credibility
- To negotiate a coaching agreement
- To determine whether you want to form a partnership with this person
- To sign a coaching agreement and receive a cheque

Your presentation

Now that you have an appointment, you must prepare and make your presentation. A good presentation will appeal to all three communications receptors. i.e. eyes, ears and sensation. We highly recommend the I CAN presentation, but you can develop your own. A typical presentation for people wanting to transform their lives includes:

The pace of life: Most people have little time even to think about the future in any clear terms and have opted to see what happens next. The safest way to predict the future is to create it.

Creating your own future is possible when you know what you want, write it down, develop a plan to get there, overcome the psychological road blocks in your way, manage your emotions, your time, your relationships and solve your own problems.

Why we don't do it: Procrastination, stress, fear, doubt, guilt, insecurity and lack of motivation are among a few reasons why most people have not designed their own future.

Can coaching help? Yes! It helps athletes, business managers and millions of individuals to achieve their goals.

What is life coaching? A partnership aimed at bringing the best out of you for the purpose of achieving your goals. Assistance with designing your future, balancing your life, making decisions, solving problems and getting results.

What can you expect

from our life coach?

Total confidentiality, a strategic approach,

honesty, non-judgemental, will never make decisions for you, faith in you and respect for your values.

What does it cost? Our coaching system is made up of 12 units. In each we discuss various aspects of your life to develop a winning strategy. Each unit costs £?? + extras, .i.e. telephone support or research. The units are split into 3 modules and can only be purchased in modular form. You may purchase module 1 as a tester. If satisfied, you can go on to modules 2 and 3.

Overcoming objections

If a prospect declines or asks for time, it usually means that they have a hidden objection. Of course, some are very helpful and will tell you up front where their objection lies; but most would not. You should familiarise yourself with every conceivable objection and develop a strategy for overcoming them. The typical objections are:

I don't need it	Is that because you have already designed your future or because you don't care?
I can't afford it	The cost of designing your future may run into hundreds but the cost of not doing it will run into thousands.
I don't like you	Is it me? Think of me as a postman and then focus on the post.
I don't believe in you	Take a test module and I'll refund you the money if you are not fully satisfied

I must be weak if I need a coach

That would make Mike Tyson , Evandor Holllyfield and Lennox Lewis weak also. Employing a coach is a mark of strength not weakness.

Closing ratios

From generating interest to closing the sale may take days, weeks or even months. You may even begin with a close ratio of 10 -1. That means you closed only one out of 10 presentations. Your close ratio will increase with practise and as your reputation for giving a first class service grows. The important thing is to overcome the fear of rejection and continue searching for your next customer.

The close

The purpose of every sales presentation is to generate a sale. A cheque and a signature is what you are looking for when all is said and done. When the presentation is finished, the wrong thing to say is:

'Well, what do you think?' The golden rule in sales is that you get what you ask for if you ask wisely. If you want a signature and cheque, whip out the standard agreement and ask for both.

Chapter 12
Compliances

Choosing a legal structure

As a professional life coach you will need to select a suitable legal structure for your new venture. At first you may start off as:

A sole trader
you can start right away without registering with any government agency. You only have to:

- Print your own stationary
- Open a bank account
- Start marketing, advertising and promoting
- your services.
- Get an accountant to register you with the Inland Revenue and to complete your annual returns.

As a sole trader you are responsible for:

- Keeping accurate records of all your sales and purchases.
- Keeping and filing all receipts for any business

related expenses.
- Employing an accountant to file your annual returns or doing it yourself.

NB: The money spent running your business will not be taxed; but what ever is left over will be taxed at the highest possible rate, which can be 60% for high earners.

The liabilities of sole trader status are that:

- You may pay more taxes
- You are personally liable for the company's debts
- You are personally liable for claims against the company
- You and your company are one

Private company limited by shares

These companies usually end with Ltd. As such, you may own the company and be employed by it; but you are not the company and have limited your liability in respect to the company's debts and claims against it to an agreed amount, usually not exceeding £100.00.
The benefits of using a limited company are:

- Your personal liability is limited
- There are more ways to save taxes using a Ltd company
- The limited company is considered more prestigious than a sole trader

As a private Ltd company director, it is your responsibility to:

- Form the company and register it at Companies House (this can be done by a formation agent)
- Keep all statutory documents in order
- File all company resolutions and decisions with Companies House
- Operate at all times in the interests of the company and not of yourself
- Submit audited accounts and an annual return to Companies House

The main down sides in operating as a limited company are:

- Meticulous paper work
- Your company's records are public and published on the internet

Finally, you may consider becoming a

private company limited by guarantee

Such companies may end in Ltd but don't have to. They are effectively 'not for profit' companies. This means that all the profits should be ploughed back into the company, used to start other companies or donated to charity. They cannot be shared out amongst owners in the form of dividends. All of the benefits and liabilities of limited status apply, with the addition that companies limited by guarantee may enjoy tax benefits in the form of reduced business rates, etc.

Using disclaimers

It is possible that a client may blame you for a particular outcome in their life. They may claim that the outcome is as a direct result of your advice. They may even attempt to bring a legal action against you. For that reason you should include and explain a disclaimer in your standard coaching agreement. A standard disclaimer reads like this:

I Jane do fully understand that
I alone am responsible for any outcomes of the coaching relationship
Coach has not guaranteed any outcome of the coaching relationship
I alone am responsible for my own decisions

Signed: Jane   Date:_____

Liability insurance

It may be wise to seek liability insurance for your practise. However, coaching is still the new kid on the block and insurance companies will watch it carefully before underwriting policies.

Self-employed

Welcome to the world of self-employment; annual returns, book keeping, receipts and invoices, marketing, advertising, presenting and selling. Get used to it,

because it will be your life from here on. The beautiful thing is that you get to determine your own income by the goals you set for yourself. If your close ratio is 10 -1, you would need to make 100 presentations in order to get 10 clients. However, the miracle is that your ten clients will each give you five leads of which at least two will yield sales. You have now gone from 10 to 30 clients in total. Each of your 20 new clients will give you five leads of which an average of two will work. So now you have 40 new clients and have coached 70 people through their life changes. You get the picture? Eventually you will catch some big fish that are willing to pay top money for exclusive services. Get five of these in your clientele and you may be a full time coach for life!
Go for it!

Conclusion

This book is designed to give you some idea of what it means to become a professional life coach. Of course, if this book was enough, many more people would be in the business of enriching others. The truth is that this book is only an introduction to an evolving field of work and although it is a good introduction, if I may say so myself, it is by no means the last word. In fact, the more you learn in this field, the more there is to learn. My advice then is to become a learning addict and get ahead of the others by staying in touch with the numerous trends, perspectives and developments in the coaching business. This is about the only way to guarantee your success as a life coach.

I'm going to make some recommendations that I strongly believe will accelerate your success as a professional life coach.

Do a course in coaching (like the one I offer on my website). There is no substitute for joining in with others on the journey, doing some role play and being able to directly interact with your teacher. Courses that are fully accredited by reputable universities are always a good idea. However, accreditation is by no means a guarantee of work. In fact, most of today's highest paid life coaches have never done an accredited course in coaching. What will make the difference for you is REFERALS from satisfied customers.

Attend seminars on various aspects of coaching and personal change techniques. NLP has become the most popular perspective on coaching. It is certainly not the only one and by its own admission is a salad of various streams of psychology. I do recommend some NLP training as it does analyse human behaviour in insightful ways and offers a plethora of tools for helping your clients to make those important transitions.

Read as many as 100 books by experts in your field. Books are fabulous because they often summarise and condense years of research and experience into one easy to read volume. If you read and understand fifty books on any given subject you would be able to speak with authority on that subject. But when you read 100 or more, you are becoming an expert. By the way, experts get paid more. So if you want to go full time in this business, developing expertise in your coaching niche is the sure way to do it.

Listen to audio books and programmes on all aspects of business, leadership, sales, marketing and life management. We live in the MP3 age. This means that we can carry around with us literally hours of listening. Unfortunately most of that listening is music that accompanies us during travel time. You can convert your travel time into learning time by downloading audio books and programmes of your coaching niche.

Join a coaching association and benefit from contacts, updates and opportunities in your niche. In fact, whatever your niche, join the relevant associations as they can be a great source of business.

Attend exhibitions in your field. Of course, you should go with business cards in hand; but you should also go to learn and to discover. Most exhibitions host seminars and provide plenty of networking opportunities to advance your business. Find out when and where they are and don't miss them. If you can also afford to exhibit, all the better; but if not, you may still make the most of the occasion.

Develop an effective website. When people want to know about you they simply look at your website. No website – no business!

Get the companion book to this one entitled 'GET PAID,' and go through it with a fine tooth comb. It is packed with frank tips and ideas for selling yourself and even for bypassing the big boys in your field.

I wish you every success in the world and I hope to see you at one of my coaching courses.

Wayne

Bonus Chapter 12
From the Critical Skills Coaching Series

Problem Solving

NB: I am including this bonus chapter on problem solving from my book 'the science of bespoke living' and the Critical Skills Coaching home study system because it contains some important concepts for both coaches and clients. You can use this lesson personally or professionally as a practising life coach. More than anything, I hope you will draw from it an invincible attitude that gives you and your clients the edge in life and in business.

The problem solver!

You are in the problem solving business. In fact, there isn't any other kind of business. All businesses exist to provide systematic solutions to specific problems. Entrepreneurs are simply problem solvers. The difference is that they have moved on from the ordinary task of solving their own problems and into the full time business of solving other people's. They provide business and consumer solutions in exchange for money. They are nothing more than professional problem solvers.

How much they are paid depends on two main factors:

Firstly, how large or complicated the problem is. The more complex the problem, the more pay for the man who can come up with a reliable and systematic solution.

Secondly, how many people share the same problem. If lots of people are experiencing the same problem, then lots of people are willing to pay for the solution. Entrepreneurs love problems because they know that the starting point of every profitable idea or innovation is fundamentally a problem or need. They need a problem in order to start a business and are consequently on the lookout for them.

A precious secret

Once Alexander the great had conquered the known world, he literally sat down and cried because there was no place left to conquer. If every problem in the world were solved today, the entrepreneurs would cry also because they would no longer be able to utilise and get paid for their problem solving skills. This is one of life's most profound and precious secrets. The reason why the rich get richer and the poor get poorer is because of the different ways in which they view problems. The rich view problems as opportunities, whilst the poor views them as obstacles. Of course I am referring to the rich who acquired their riches through hard work and to the poor who have made nothing of the many opportunities that life brought their way.

In reality poverty and wealth have more to do with your mental state than with a healthy bank balance. A poor mentality is one that sees problems as setbacks and obstacles, whilst a rich mentality sees those same problems as set-ups and opportunities. Again I say that this idea constitutes one of life's most sacred mysteries. The reason why wealth is so disproportionately distributed in the world is because human nature seeks to avoid problems. Most people are running away from their problems. They hate them and are busy running with money in hand to the person who has a solution.

They are running towards those few people who realise that necessity is the mother of invention and that problems are the seeds of great ideas and that solutions always sell well. Those few are the elite 10% who see opportunities in problems and get to enjoy 90% of the world's wealth.

Whatever business field or profession you are in, remember that it's existence is only justified by the problems it solves. Imagine, if there were no sick or dying people in the world, we would not be able to justify the existence of a medical profession. If there were no crimes or legal disputes in the world, lawyers and judges, courts and prisons would all go out of business. The same principle holds true of your role within your industry. Your place in the company is only justified by the problems you solve for the company.

You are being paid then to solve problems. The amount you are paid reflects the scale of the problem that you solve for the company. The more complex the problem, the more you get paid for solving it. The less complex the problem, the less you get paid for solving it. Your position and your pay are only justified by the scale of the problems you solve. If you want to get more pay, simply make it your business to acquire the advance knowledge and skills necessary to solve the more complex problems within your field. If you have not already figured it out, wake up now and smell the coffee! You are not being paid for your work; you are being paid for your results!

The universe agrees

The same principle holds true in the universe. Every single atom in the universe solves a specific problem within its own molecule. Everything that God ever made solves a unique problem for something else, because we live in an interdependent universe in which everything is dependant upon something else for its existence and sustenance. The earth needs the sun and the soil needs the rain and the birds need the air and the fish need the sea and so on and so on. Literally everything in the universe is solving a problem for something else in the universe.

The same is true of human inventions. Everything that man ever made was made to solve a problem. My laptop is solving a problem for me right now and I know that eventually my publishers will solve a problem for both of us by converting my notes into a book and making it available to you. Houses, furniture, décor, cars, streets and shops all solve problems.

Serving a purpose

There is no difference between solving a problem and serving a purpose. Things that solve problems serve purposes, and things that don't solve don't serve. This principle holds true for you personally and for your business of life. Your life only serves a purpose in as much as it solves a problem and just like everything else in the universe, your very existence is justified by the problems you solve. Settle it in your mind that you are a problem solver and that problem solving is your main business in life.

Whoever heard of a fireman that ran away from fires? Or a plumber who avoided drains and broken pipes? It's ludicrous! It is equally ludicrous for purpose built problem solvers like you to run away from problems. You are a purpose built problem solver and solving problems is your speciality. Of course you need some tools and that is my purpose in this chapter. However, more than any tool or technique, you need an invincible attitude. Problem solving starts with an invincible attitude that emanates from your beliefs about problems. So what do you believe about problems?

The most effective and successful people in the world share common ideas and beliefs about problems.

Problems are inevitable: It is simply naive to think that you can walk through life or embark upon a project without some problem cropping up. In fact the ability to anticipate problems is one of the key skills necessary to solving them. Many project managers and entrepreneurs operate by Murphy's Law which effectively says that anything that can go wrong will go wrong, and the worst possible thing that can go wrong will go wrong at the worst possible time. This law is designed to take the naivety out of the planning process, so that planners can anticipate problems and develop solutions to them before they arrive, if not avoiding them altogether. But isn't Murphy's Law rather negative? No! Anticipating problems is only negative if you use it to justify procrastination or non-progression. If on the other hand you use it to develop advanced solutions, then it is nothing short of skilful.

Problems are solvable: There is a solution to every problem. Just because the answer isn't obvious does not mean it is not there. Just because you have never seen a black swan does not mean they don't exist. Just because nobody has ever done it before does not mean it can't be done. What you believe about the solvability of a problem will determine how hard you look for a solution. If you don't believe that a particular problem can be solved, you are hardly going to look for a solution. If on the other hand you believe that it can and must be solved, you will not stop seeking that solution till you find it. Thomas Edison invented the electric light bulb after 10,000 failed attempts. He treated each failure as a learning curve. What do you think kept him going in spite of 10,000 failures? His belief that the problem was solvable!

Problems are beneficial: There is a mysterious blessing hidden in every problem you face. The gift of power always comes securely wrapped up in a problem. If you solve the problem you get the power. It's that simple. Problem solvers become more powerful with each problem they solve because in the process they acquire new knowledge and skills. With each victory, their self-esteem rises and with it their confidence. It is as though your hidden potential and creative genius is sleeping inside of you waiting for a problem of sufficient magnitude to come along and wake up the super man within you. There is a glorious purpose for every problem you face. When you understand the purpose of the problem, you can harness the power of the problem. The threefold purpose of your problems are as follows:

To Squeeze Out Hidden Potential: Hidden in you are the most incredible capabilities, concepts and creativity; but your inner genius will never be known until the right kind of pressure forces and squeezes it out. When a baby is born, we know that it is more than a bundle of fun and that it is also a bundle of potential. We therefore create systems and institutions designed to get that potential out. One such institution is school. For the child, school, maths and homework are one big problem. But we don't feel sorry for the child because we know that the pressure is squeezing out a genius. In the same way, your problems serve to bring out of you a new level of competence, concept and creativity that you would not have otherwise known.

To Motivate You: There are only two great motivators in life - **pain and pleasure**. Whenever we get lethargic, lazy, casual or indifferent in our attitude towards progress, problems come along with so much pain attached that we are instantly motivated to get on with our plans and stop wasting time. In this way, problems can strengthen your resolve to achieve your goals and live your dreams. They may feed your faith, strengthen your beliefs and reinforce your personal philosophy. There are some moves you will never make in life until the pain of staying put outweighs the potential pain of taking action.

To Educate You: In the process of solving a problem, you will acquire new knowledge and skills. You will discover things you didn't know. Often the problems will drive you to the library or to the Internet or to an expert to get information that you would otherwise not even have been interested in. In this way the problem will educate you.

Problem leverage

When problems pop up along your way, your first thought is to leverage from it and asking the question 'why?' Is it here to squeeze out my hidden potential? Is it here to motivate me? Is it here to educate me? When you work out why life has so graciously given to you this amazing opportunity, you simply begin to flow in that direction. For example, if you work out that this problem has come to educate you, go ahead and be educated. If you conclude that it is here to motivate you, just go ahead and be motivated by it. If it is here to squeeze out your hidden potential, just go ahead and be creative with it. By doing this, you ensure that you never go through the problem, but that you always grow through the problem.

Problem solving starts with an invincible attitude based on a belief system that won't take no for an answer. However, the attitude alone without skill will only take you part of the way. Hopefully, by now I have armed you with sufficient evidence that any problem can be solved and that you are purpose built to solve them; but now I want to focus on the necessary skills for getting the job done.

What's the problem anyway?

Let us start by defining the word 'problem.' Anything that hinders your progress towards a particular goal is a problem. We are far too quick to label the things that irritate, aggravate, frustrate and upset us as problems. However, if they do not actually prevent you from going about your business, they are not really problems. For some people, the alarm clock going off in the morning is a problem. However, in the context of this lesson it simply does not qualify. They have confused natural life experiences with problems. Just because it irritates you or is uncomfortable does not earn it the right to be called a problem. It is just life. To earn the label 'problem', it must literally act as a roadblock in your way by actually preventing you from making the progress you intended or from taking a necessary action. It may be a material obstacle in your way, i.e. 'the sponsor has pulled out' or 'the client refuses to pay', etc. Or it could be an emotional roadblock where somebody's behaviour has left you in an utterly un- resourceful state where you can't function normally. Whatever the case, it is not a problem until you have to deal with it in order to move on.

Potential problems

Anything that threatens to hinder your progress is a **potential problem.** That means it has the potential to stop you in your tracks, but is not doing so as yet. Very often people react to potential problems as if they were present problems and bring their plans to a grinding halt even though nothing is actually preventing them from making progress.

Perceived problems

Any **impotent obstacle** in your way is a perceived problem. Impotent obstacles can be quiet vocals; but when examined prove to be powerless in the fight against your progress. I personally view impotent obstacles as cartoon characters - large, loud and colourful; but possessing no power in the real world.

Make the distinction

The rule is that real problems should be solved by remedial action; potential problems should be arrested through preventative action and perceived problems should be ignored and left behind. Any failure to make these necessary distinctions will lead to unnecessary stress and the implementation of ineffective strategies. For example, some people believe that if you ignore a problem it will eventually go away or work itself out. However, this is only true of perceived problems. If you ignore present or potential problems they will simply get worse and ultimately derail your destiny. Likewise, if you treat potential problems as if they were present, you may freeze in your tracks when nothing is actually preventing you from making progress.

If you were attempting to buy a property but found out that you are £5000.00 short of your deposit, you would have an immediate problem, in that there is a material obstacle standing in your way. This is not a potential or perceived problem. You simply cannot go forward until you have solved it.

Only three things you can do

There are only three things you can do to solve a problem. You eliminate it so that it no longer exists or you bypass it, having found an alternative route to achieving your goals or you fasten your seat belt and go through it until the turbulence ceases. Move it, go around it or go through it! In this instant you eliminate the problem by finding the necessary £5000.00 from another source or you circumvent the problem by finding another lender who is willing to work with the deposit you have or you buckle down, give this property a miss and save the additional £5000.00 over a period of time.

If you are buying a piece of real estate and then hear that someone else has made a better offer on that property, you might have a potential problem on your hands. Your job now is to prevent it from becoming a problem. You do this by creating problems for the problem. You literally put obstacles in it's way in order to prevent it from becoming an obstacle in your way. In this case you should first seek to verify the claim; at which point you may seek to get the property taken off the market or you may try to win over the vendor or even in some cases to dissuade your competitor. However, what you don't do is freeze, slow down or pull out over information that may not even be true.

If you are buying that piece of real estate and an interested party starts to sniff around the property but has made no formal offer as yet, you don't actually have a problem at all. It is not time to get worked up or even concerned. There is no problem except the one you perceive. Don't waste another metal mega byte on problems that don't even exist.

Perception equals reality

How you react to the appearance of a problem may prove a bigger problem than the problem itself. Remember, life has no meaning apart from the ones you give to it. In this respect, there is no difference between your perception and your reality. The events and the occurrences in your life have absolutely no power to shape your destiny apart from the meanings that you attach to them. The real problem then is in your perception of the situation and not in the situation itself. The real problem is not what happens, but what you make of it and how you deal with it. The real issue is whether you see an obstacle or an opportunity in the problem at hand. So let's first consider some of the most ineffective, yet popular ways that people look at and handle problems:

Shock: There is no such thing as a fool-proof plan. Anything can happen; and if anything can happen, something will happen. Don't be naïve; anticipate it and predetermine your strategy for dealing with it.

Ignore It: Some people think that if they ignore a problem, it will eventually sort itself out and go away. This happens with perceived problems; but not with present or potential problems. The more you ignore them, the worse they become.

Focus On It: Some people get so completely embroiled in their problems until they lose sight of their purpose, plan and progress to date. You should focus on solutions and not problems. You should aim to become solution and result orientated, not problem and obstacle orientated.

Fear: Don't panic when a problem occurs. The fear alone will do more damage to your plans than the problem itself ever could. Fear is more dangerous than the thing you fear. Panic paralyses! Instead, realise that there is a solution to this problem even if it is not obvious at the moment. The fact that others have made it to where you are heading is living proof that it can be done.

Surrender! If failure is an option to you, then problems will secure the death of your dreams. You must rule out the possibility of failure or retreat. You must never surrender to a problem. Never surrender to an obstacle. In the words of Sir Winston Churchill, 'NEVER GIVE UP!'

No doubt we are all guilty of responding in one or all of these ways to the appearance of a problem. However, few problems are ever solved by these knee jerk reactions that are usually charged with emotion. If you are going to solve the problem and move on, you have to rise above some of the emotionalism attached to it and employ an effective strategy for dealing with it.

Emotions

But I hear you say, 'what if I am emotionally attached? How can I think objectively about something to which I am emotionally attached?' That is where friends, mentors, coaches and professional advisors come in. There are some problems you just cannot deal with by yourself and will have to harness the power of others in the form of a mastermind group, or some professional advice. A mastermind group consists of people who are willing to put their minds together in order to advance a particular cause. Your professional advisors include lawyers, accountants, coaches, consultants, etc. Sometimes the help comes from family and friends and at other times it comes from colleagues, mentors and associates. The Bible says, 'in the multitude of counsellors there is safety.'

It is simply a waste of mind power to spend three days racking your brains over a problem that could have been solved by one phone call to your lawyer. Likewise it should take three minds approximately one third of the time that it would take one mind to solve any particular problem. However in practise it turns out that two additional minds may accelerate the process by as much as six times so that 3 people may find a solution in one hour that may other wise have taken one man six hours to find, if he would find it at all. The lesson here is that you should make full use of your personal network when confronting problems and not waste unnecessary time and energy confronting them alone.

The 8 D formula for solving problems:

The following represents a framework for dealing with problems and can be used by individuals or groups who come together to confront problems. I call it the 8D solution because it focuses on 8 D's. It may be helpful to do this as a small group particularly if you feel emotionally attached to the situation. Caution! In order to do this effectively you must do it on paper!

Define It: In a nutshell, what is the problem? Define it by just a one-liner or two-liner. Why? A problem defined is a problem half solved. Fifty percent of the problem is defining it.

Describe It: How exactly is it hindering your progress? What are its causes, effects and symptoms? Write just a few lines on this one. Why? Because it will become clear at that point exactly why you can't live with it, dither or procrastinate any further. You must get rid of it now.

Detach It: Put it in perspective. It is not your whole life. Don't become absorbed by it to the point of depression. Isolate it and celebrate all the good things happening in your life. Why? You will become fearful if you perceive the problem to be bigger than it is.

Doubt It: Don't doubt your destiny; doubt your doubts! Question the problem as though it were a person you did not trust or believe. Disbelieve its claims and refuse to listen to its propaganda. Why? Problems present themselves as invincible. You must not believe this but rather firmly maintain that there is a way through this.

Determine Your Desired Outcome: What do you want? How would you like this to be resolved? List three possible outcomes that you would be prepared to accept. List them as 1st, 2nd and 3rd choice. Why? Up until this point, your focus was the problem. When you decide what you want, you have effectively established a goal. You now know what you are aiming for and can create a pathway to it. You can now focus on the solution in a way that you could not before this point. The first step in getting where you want to go is knowing where you want to go. This is the great turning point in your problem solving process and the master key to designing a solution.

Design A Solution: You are now ready to map out all the possible routes to your chosen destination. There will be a number of pathways that lead to your 1st, 2nd and 3rd choices. Instead of choosing one of these paths, employ the best features of them all to get you where you want to go. Be flexible, not rigid!

Deal With It: Designing a solution does not deal with the problem. Implementing your solution does.

Document It: Monitor your progress using a journal. In days to come it will be a great source of inspiration and education for you and others.

Ignorance is the problem

A bolder in the road is only an obstacle to the person who doesn't know how to move it and who has no alternative route. Likewise, your own personal and professional problems are only ever obstacles if you don't know how to solve them. In this respect, the only real problem is your lack of knowledge in that area. This rule can be applied to virtually any problem. **'I can't'** always means **'I don't know how'**. 'We can't' always means 'We don't know how.' Centuries ago we couldn't make light without fire; we couldn't whisper to another person who was thousands of miles away and have every word heard with perfect clarity; we couldn't stand on the moon; we couldn't heat a meal without fire; we couldn't get from Britain to America without sailing, etc..; but time has proven that we simply didn't know how. Based on this fact alone you should cease thinking in terms of 'I can't' and start thinking in terms of 'I don't know how.' You should immediately stop saying 'I cannot' and instead start asking 'how can I?' The next time a problem pops up, ask yourself the kind of questions that stimulate your creative mind. These are the how questions like – 'how can I overcome this obstacle? How can I turn this circumstance into an opportunity? How can I leverage from this situation? How can I eliminate this obstruction? How can I circumnavigate this roadblock? Etc...'

The magic question

Your subconscious mind is obligated to find an answer to the **'how can I'** question, but only if it is repeated often enough. Jesus said - 'ask and it shall be given unto you, seek and you shall find, knock and it shall be opened unto you.' These words were originally written in a Greek tense which suggests, 'continue asking and it shall be given unto you, continue seeking, continue knocking. Great inventors are simply those people who continued asking the question how? Great innovators are those who continue asking the question how? Great problem solvers are simply those who compelled a solution into being by consistently asking the all important question **'how?'**

The 'how' question stimulates your creative brain to rapidly process a series of potential solutions. This process happens much faster than your conscious mind can keep up with and even continues working while you are asleep. This is how Eureka's are born. When you put two or more additional minds into the mix, the process is further accelerated to extraordinary levels. This is because two or more minds asking the how question, with the same level of intensity creates the mastermind phenomenon. This phenomenon is others wise known as super intelligence. Mental chemistry is the most potent force available to man for forging his own future. Jesus said - 'if two or three of you agree as touching anything that you ask in my name, it shall be done.' There are very few problems man will ever face that can withstand the power of two or three minds dedicated to overcoming it. Your job then is to harness the power of accelerated thought by bringing one or two others on board when facing a real stubborn problem.

Brain storming

It is a waste of time and energy to try to deal with these tough cookies alone. Get a group together and say 'friends, this is the problem. Will you help me find a solution?' You can then employ the 8D formula together or go straight to brainstorming. You brain storm by asking every one in your group to come up with as many possible solutions or acceptable outcomes as possible. Just go around the table and let the ideas flow. Don't stop until you have at least 20 potential solutions; but go for a hundred. You must have somebody write down all the solutions offered whilst resisting the temptation to comment on any of them until the very end, even if some sound stupid. The exercise is designed to get your creative juices flowing and to create mental chemistry within your mastermind group. In order to do this, each person must begin offering solutions, no matter how ludicrous they may sound at first. They will eventually become sound and weighty with each new attempt. This method virtually guarantees a solution to any problems you face personally or professionally because it utilises the only tool that God gave you for solving problems, namely your magnificent mind.

Get professional advice

Another waste of time and energy is worrying about something outside your circle of knowledge. If the situation requires professional, legal or financial advise, don't hesitate to get it. A professional advisor could save you days and months of research and may not cost as much as it may seem. Initial consultations are usually free. You should be able to gauge whether the situation can be resolved through an intervention on the professional level. At the very least you should come out wiser, having obtained more options to add to your list.

Coaching Carts

The Wheel of Life

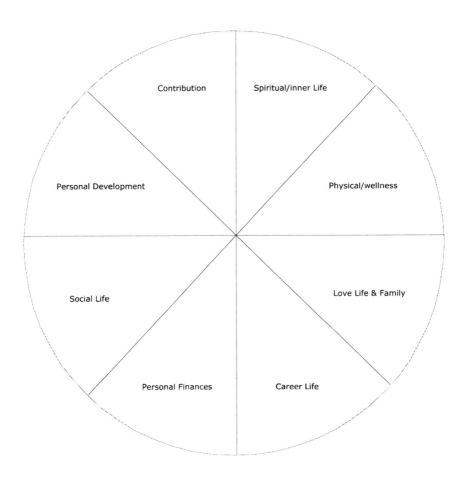

Design-a-day!

Write in the boxes

Outlook
How will you sustain a
positive mental attitude

Inputs
What will you eat? How will you
exercise? How will you rest?

Outputs
List your tasks

Outcomes
How would you like the day to end?

Aim to Live!

Goals	Short Range 6 Months - 1 year	Mid Range 1 year - 3 years	Long Range 3 years - 5 years
Spiritual Inner life			
Personal health, fitness, hobbies, growth,			
Social Friends, family, recreation			
Financial Career, personal finances			

Life Zone_____

My Goal
Write in the boxes

What	Why
How	When
With what	With who
Cost	Benefit

Shifting Gears

G GOAL	
E EXPLORE	
A ACTION	
R REASONS	
S SUCCESS	

T-GROW

T THEME	What would you like to talk about today?
G GOAL	What do you want in this area?
R REASONS	What will that do for you?
O OPTIONS	How many options are available to you?
W WAY FORWARD	Which of these options is the best way forward?

The Coaching Arrow

A AIMS	What am I aiming for?
R REALITY	What are the realities of my present situation?
R REASONS	What is my compelling reason for pursuing this goal?
O OPTIONS	What are the options available to me?
W WAY FORWARD	Which way leads forward?

Simply The Best
COACHING SYSTEM

A breakthrough in Personal Development

THIS PROGRAMME COMES COMPLETE WITH 16 CD'S INCLUDING:

- *12 Audio Books*
- *Transcripts*
- *Coaching Templates*
- *Over 700 articles on Personal Development*

  and more!...

'Life gets simple when you get smart!'

Order the complete system today at
www.bestcoachingsystem.co.uk

LaVergne, TN USA
10 February 2010
172641LV00002B/68/P